WINNING DIGITAL WAY

MARKETING MADE SIMPLE

ANISH K RAVI

For Papa

(26 February 1949 – 14 September 2021)

Contents

Contents

Preface

Rapid digitalization affects all aspects of life - including how we interact, work, shop, and receive services - and how value is created and exchanged. Data and cross-border data flows are becoming increasingly crucial to development in this process. It is estimated that the world's digital economy is growing at 10% per year. The impact of digital technology has been referred to as the Third Industrial Revolution.

How has this revolution impacted business?

Digital transformation is being used to change customer relationships, internal processes, and the value propositions we can deliver.

My focus in this book is the impact of digital technology on the marketing function. There is little doubt that digital technologies have substantially impacted marketing. Organizations now have more data, marketing formats, and online places to communicate with consumers, including social networks, blogs, search engines, YouTube videos, etc. How well is the marketing function within your organization embracing digital technology and effectively leveraging its opportunities? And more importantly, how ready are you to understand digital transformation and make strategic decisions to apply effective digital marketing in the workplace? Marketing needs digitally savvy practitioners who can also use a strategic and systematic approach to digital marketing.

It has been a quarter-century since the commercial use of the Internet, and the World Wide Web began. During that time, the business landscape has changed at a frenetic pace. Large multinational corporations such as Alphabet (Google), Facebook, Amazon, and Alibaba, all of which were unheard of twenty-five years ago, have emerged as critical players in our modern economy. Online sales have been increasing steadily, sometimes at the expense of offline sales. The market size of the online retail industry in India amounted to approximately 60 billion U.S. dollars in 2020. It showed an increasing trend since 2015. The online retail industry was forecasted to reach 73 billion U.S. dollars by 2022. Sales made through mobile devices have increased rapidly to around 22% - 40% of all online sales.

Corporations now highlight the importance of creating a "Digital Relationship" with customers. Moreover, digital technologies and devices such as smartphones, innovative products, the Internet of Things (IoT), Artificial Intelligence, and Deep Learning promise significant transformations in consumers‘ lives in the coming years.

Against this backdrop, the book will help you understand how the developments in digital technology are re-shaping the process and the strategy of marketing in the broad space we call "DIGITAL MARKETING". This book offers an extensive overview of the foundation of digital marketing by providing a mix of strategy and implementation tools.

First, the book explores the various touchpoints in marketing and understands how emerging digital technologies will impact marketing.

Second, the book will provide specifics on using digital platforms, focusing on outbound and inbound marketing, social media, and mobile platforms to interact with consumers, understand the acquisition and retention costs, and use digital marketing most efficiently.

Third, the book prepares you to anticipate how innovations in technology are likely to impact the digital marketing landscape and help you analyze the impact on the business, and design marketing plans accordingly.

It is, of course, difficult to ignore the pandemic and its impact on digital adoption by consumers, who have vaulted five years in the digital adoption curve in just a few weeks. I will put forth my observations on the effect of this shock on digital marketing as a whole – from the consumers' perspective and the firms' perspective.

Acknowledgements

I want to thank everyone who ever said anything positive to me or taught me something. I heard it all, and it meant something.

I want to thank God most of all because I wouldn't be able to do any of this without God.

CHAPTER I

Potted History of The Internet

Digital Marketing revolves around the Internet. But what is the Internet? I would like you to explore the history and evolution of the Internet. The Internet is the physical network that underpins the World Wide Web and, therefore, the online or digital marketing platform. As marketers, it is helpful to understand the history and evolution of the Internet. There is so much internet history that I couldn't get to everything in this book, so I will have to write a second one. Anyway, let's get started.

The Internet started over 50 years ago, and computers back then filled up entire rooms. Scientists and researchers used it for years to communicate during the Cold War. It was helpful because if one computer went down, the others wouldn't follow. In 1962 a scientist named JCR Licklider proposed the idea of a network of computers that could talk to one another. In 1969 the first-ever message was sent from one computer to another over the ARPANET, the government's computer network at the time. ARPANET stands for Advanced Research Projects Agency, located in a research lab in UCLA and the other at Stanford. All the message said was log in, and it didn't fail to crash the network. Stanford only received the first two letters of the note, but hey, you have to start somewhere. Only four computers were connected to this network by the end of the year.

In 1971 the University of Hawaii's ALOHAnet was added, followed by various networks in London and Norway two years later. Also, in 1971 Ray Tomlinson developed the first system to send mail back and forth between the users of ARPAnet, which would eventually be called electronic mail or email for short. The @ symbol was used to tell a person's name and the hostname; apart from all of the networks floating around, there needed to be a way for all of the computers to communicate with other networks, and this is where a computer scientist named Vinton Cerf comes in. He invented a way to introduce computers across the globe to each other in a virtual space. This invention was called transmission control protocol or TCP, followed by Internet Protocol or IP. In the 80s, scientists used Cerf's protocol to send data back and forth, but the 90s is where it all began. In 1991 computer programmer named Tim Berners-Lee invented the World Wide Web, which wasn't just a data-sharing space for scientists anymore; this was an entire network of information accessible to anyone with an internet connection. I am sure you use internet browsers, and some of the popular ones are Firefox, Google Chrome, and Safari. But in 1992, Erwise was created. Erwise was an internet browser and the first to have a graphical interface. A few browsers came before and after, but in 1993 Mosaic was made, and it would popularize surfing the web. Mosaic influenced many browsers to follow, including Netscape Navigator in 1994, and became the most popular web browser, accounting for 90% of the web usage in 1995.

In the early 90s, companies like AOL and CompuServe started providing dial-up internet access. Dial-up is a method of connecting to the Internet via a telephone line. There was a period in history when you couldn't use your telephone and the Internet simultaneously. Without the Internet, we obviously wouldn't have things like Facebook, Twitter, and YouTube, but, way, more importantly, we wouldn't be able to access information in seconds. We wouldn't be able to communicate with people worldwide, share ideas and educate those who might not get a chance elsewhere. Also, without the Internet, I would have to talk to someone when I order a pizza, which was the first thing ever purchased on the Internet. How would your life be different without the Internet?

Internet Use and Connectivity Worldwide

Recent estimates published in 2021 indicate that over 53% of the world's total population uses the Internet. Review the exhibit below to examine the Internet penetration rate for each region and its relative contribution to Internet users worldwide.

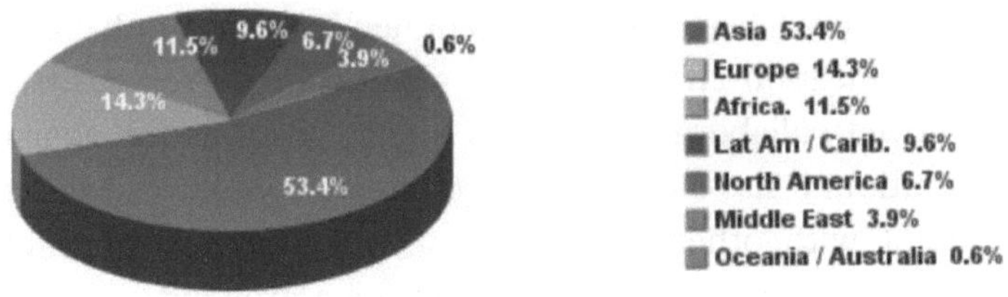

Internet World Stats

Web 2.0: A Game Changer

The evolution of the Web has dictated how we publish and access information on the Internet. Web 1.0 generally refers to the Web when it was a set of static websites with no interactive content. In Web 1.0, applications were usually owned. Around 2004, the next phase of the Web, Web 2.0, became more prominent, and Tim O'Reilly articulated its key competencies.

Web 2.0 is often used today to define the second generation of web user interaction and design. Suppose the first generation used the Internet as a simple way to get information. In that case, the web 2.0 generation represents the movement to the Internet as an interactive platform to collaborate, develop, share, and operate simultaneously on the Web. Important Web 2.0 developments include web-based communities, hosting services, and applications like Facebook, Twitter, YouTube, and Wikipedia. The web 2.0 platform has created a stir of innovative activity in the business world. Many companies are scrambling to create an online experience for their customers and clients and learn how to harness new technologies to expand their brands, products, and influence. The evolution to Web 2.0 has delivered better network connectivity and enhanced communication channels. Most significantly, Web 2.0 has improved collaboration and, in effect, given us the social revolution. It has enabled users to create content and share content with others. Community input, interaction, and content sharing can now occur across a growing range of social media sites and applications such as forums, micro-blogging, social networking sites, and wikis.

Who's Got the Power?

The web evolution and customer adoption of new technological advancements have meant that the customers now yield a lot more power in their relationships with business. Understanding the empowered customer is essential for marketers to meet customers' changing expectations, motivations, and needs.

Forbes describes the Empowered Customer as being;

- **Mobile:** having constant access to a smartphone
- **Hands-on:** possessing more control and choices as consumers
- **Smart:** accessing multiple points of information
- **Committed:** brands must earn loyalty through delivering value and fully understanding their needs
- **Global Citizen:** accessing world markets and brands

Empowered Customer

Gone are the days of wading through back issues of magazines to figure out which washing machine is the best value. Today consumers share their opinions online on everything from their next vacation to books and big-screen TVs. When I'm researching a new car to purchase, I'm not going to go to the Maruti Suzuki website. Perhaps I'll go to blogs and discussion boards where regular people share information. I have people who have used the product talking about what they liked about it and what they didn't like. It's a way for individuals to make known their preferences in ways that really would have been impossible before. And with consumer advocacy sites, the conversation moves from consumers talking to each other to consumers demanding a two-way conversation with the companies themselves. When we suddenly have this world now where consumers have the same ability to have volume as a lot of these big corporate brands do, consumers are using that volume to get companies to stand up and listen.

Today, businesses are paying attention to what people are saying online. They monitor Twitter and other blogs to keep in touch with their customers. Any company doing it ethically is transparent and communicative, adding value to the conversation and the consumer. It is moving miles ahead of competitors. It is about a dialogue, and brands that get that and are participating are going to do well moving forward. Bottom line customers now have the tools to influence businesses to make better products, respond more quickly, and encourage them to act more responsibly.

Marketers' Response to Web 2.0

By now, you understand the expanded technologies enabled through Web 2.0 and the ensuing growth of customer empowerment. How have marketers responded to these fundamental shifts? Marketing systems have needed to change.

Marketing has undergone a transition from 'push' to 'pull' marketing, in line with technology and customer power changes. The old centralized 'push' marketing approach interrupted customers using traditional mass media. The shift in power means customers can now, for example, block advertising, source desired media content, connect with competitors around the globe, and collaborate with other customers regarding products.

Web 2.0 based technologies and customer empowerment has driven a 'pull' marketing approach. Businesses now need to focus on inbound marketing to attract or 'pull 'customers to their brand. Companies must build customer engagement and relationships through solid content by leveraging owned and earned media to reinforce difference and customer-centricity.

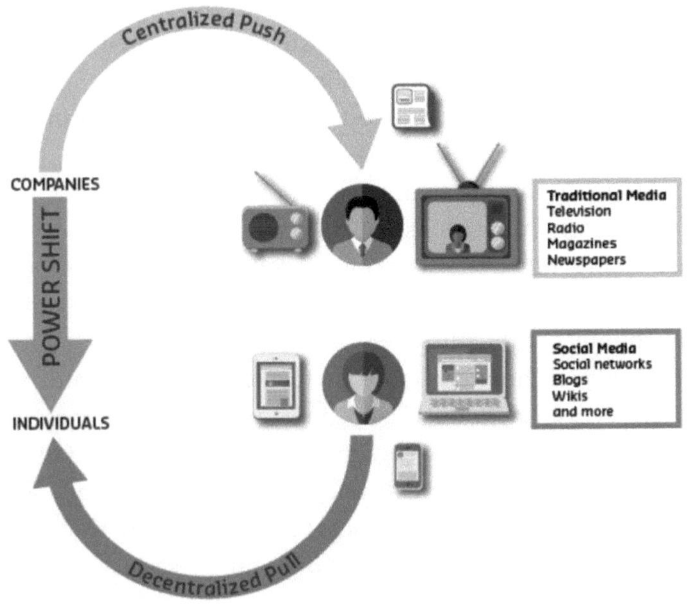

Empowered by access to more information, social networks, and digital devices, you and I as consumers have become more demanding. Many of us are increasingly skeptical about the ability of big brands to keep their promises when all of their activities, good and bad, appear in the public eye. As a result, we expect more visibility, accountability, and authenticity. They are making it more challenging for businesses to keep up.

I do think there's more information available. I think we were looking in the dark 20 years ago. Because I have access to more news, I have more enormous expectations.

When it comes to purchasing, I'm just looking for the facts instead of opinions. I expect now to shop around better using information available on the internet and ensure that I get the product I want for my needs. I always ask people or shop from the adverts and then look at reviews on the websites or online.

Businesses need to invest in developing a consumer-centric business model.

How can they do that?

Engaging with consumers needs to go beyond the marketing function. It requires collaboration across the different parts of the organization in managing the other touchpoints with consumers.

Firstly, technology and analytics can help integrate and track every individual consumer interaction across all touchpoints and channels, enabling diagnostics of failure points and guiding real-time, targeted responses. For example, you'll see a business contacting you if you've dropped out of a site when making a purchase.

Secondly, ensure staff at each level of the organization understand their role in serving consumers and empower them to make the right decision on the appropriate way to respond to dissatisfied customers. Additionally, reputational risks with social platforms need to be managed. Social command centres can be established to listen to conversations, engage with consumers, and help to share positive stories beyond the immediate consumer base to those just about to start their search for a product or brand.

Finally, content creation and management strategies should inspire and inform consumers rather than sell. Arming consumers with the correct information helps them move independently through the shopping journey. Improve their trust, and you will increase their loyalty and, ultimately, their weight of purchase.

Are Businesses Embracing New Marketing Opportunities?

McKinsey surveyed businesses worldwide, across various industries, to examine how organizations use social (Web 2.0) technologies and tools. Around 2000 businesses per year completed the survey, and it focused on 13 social technologies. The findings highlight exciting changes and trends over this period. For example:

- While there is a continuing adoption of the technologies over the timeframe, the level and rate of adoption vary significantly across different tools.

Business Perspective

Today, I think social media is so large. It's grown so large. Over the past 20 years in the industry, I've seen advertising shift from print into digital today. Any brand that wants to be relevant today and appeal to the consumer in the right segment is into digital and social media. The use of influencers today cannot be denied. The kind of exposure they can give a brand or a singular product is invaluable, you know? There are cases where a particular colour flies off the shelves in two days, just because an actress wore it in a movie.

So today, that power of the influencer is phenomenal.

CHAPTER II

Let's Call It Marketing

Before I start amplifying marketing strategy, let's understand how it has impacted the marketing function. I will also help you understand the marketing strategy formation process as it is practiced in a conventional marketing setting.

So, let's get started.

Marketing Strategy Formation Process

The marketing strategy process starts with analyzing the firm's customers‘ environment. The firm also operates within this environment, which also consists of its competitors who are targeting the same customers and collaborators for the firm, including upstream suppliers for the firm and a downstream wholesale and retail channel.

In addition, there could be other service and infrastructure providers. However, for the firm, the context specifies the geographical and cultural settings of the environment. A firm could be operating in different environments where the mix of these players could be diverse across other countries. Any firm that wants to provide its offering to a market must start by analyzing the environment in which it operates. The firm's decisions are the aspiration decisions, i.e., identifying which customer group they are creating value for with their offering.

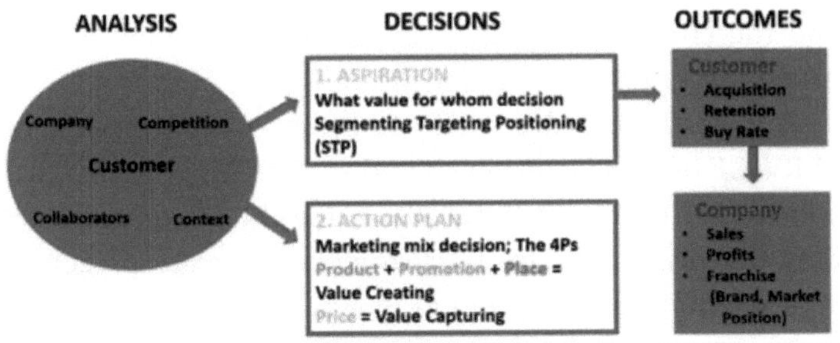

Marketing Strategy Formation Process

It leads to segmenting the market, identifying appropriate segments that the firm wants to target. And given the segments, they are targeting; they should position their offering and their brand. Typically, we use STP to refer to the Segmenting, Targeting, and Positioning decisions.

This is followed by the action plan where the firm makes its marketing mix decisions. The marketing mix consists of the four Ps of marketing: Product, Promotion, Place (distribution), and Price. Product, Promotion, and Place are the actions that create value for customers. Price is the instrument through which the firm can capture the value from customers. Now, these decisions that the company makes in terms of which segment to target, how to position its brand, and the appropriate action plans will lead to the outcomes that the firm desires. These include customer-level effects, including the increased acquisition of customers, increased retention rate, and increased purchase frequency, leading to increased revenues and profits from each customer. These customer-level outcomes lead to the company-level outcomes, which are reflected in the sales of the company, the overall profits, and the company's position in terms of its brand equity, brand recognition, and brand awareness.

The Marketing Mix itself can be seen as PRODUCT or SERVICE offering customer solution; PRICE is the cost that a customer bears, PROMOTION being the communication that the firm sends to its customers to create perceived value for their offering, and PLACE through which the firm provides convenience for customers to transact business.

Marketing Mix

As you can see, under each marketing mix heading, there are several factors or elements that are accomplished in a traditional marketing setting.

What Is Digital Marketing?

In the early years of the internet, digital marketing was narrowly conceived as promoting products and brands through electronic media. Later, as websites became ubiquitous and provided market coverage, it was seen more as a digital channel and a digital instrument to analyze firms' marketing campaigns and understand what works and what doesn't in real-time.

But digital technologies and media have exploded in number encompassing everything we do. They are everywhere.

Digital Marketing: A continuum...

From a TECHNOLOGY perspective, Digital Marketing is-

> "*Using digital technologies to acquire customers and build customer preferences, promote brands, retain customers, and increase sales.*"

From a PROCESS perspective, Digital Marketing is-

> "*An adaptive technology enabled process by which firms collaborate with customers and partners to jointly create, communicate, deliver, and sustain value for all stakeholders.*"

The adaptive process enabled by digital technologies creates values in new ways. It is facilitated by a series of adaptive digital touchpoints, encompassing the marketing activity, institutions, processes, and customers.

Having understood what digital marketing is, let's examine how digital technologies and processes have changed the marketing landscape.

CHAPTER III

Framework and Implications

Now that you have a general overview of digital marketing, let's look at the digital marketing framework. We'll look closely at the environment, which includes the customer, the context, the competitors, and the collaborators with the customer right in the middle.

Framework for Digital Marketing

We will be examining how the components of a marketing strategy formation process that we have seen before have changed due to digital technologies. This chapter will give you an overview of the framework for digital marketing that will become the basis for all my thought as we advance in this book.

It is essential to realize that much of the changes brought about by new technologies in the environment inside the company, and the outcomes can be understood using this framework. Even if some new technologies were to emerge in the future, we could use this framework to understand how the new scenario will play out.

We'll start by examining the same three concepts that we looked at in chapter one when reviewing the marketing strategy formation process.

These are the environment, marketing mix within the firm, and value creation for customers and firms.

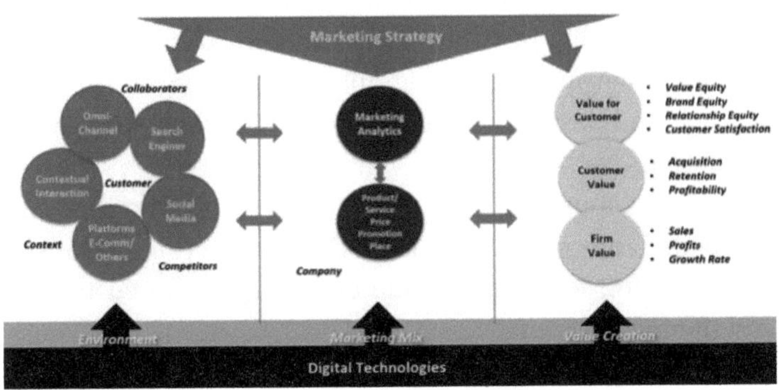

Digital Marketing Framework

As before, in the environment, we have the customer, the context, the competitors, and the collaborators with the customer right in the middle. But now have a few newer forms of institutions that have emerged in the last 25 years that have irrevocably changed the environment. The first of these is the search engines like Google, Bing, Baidu, Yandex. Platforms that connect those customers searching for information with firms using search keywords.

We have social media and chat platforms, Facebook, Instagram, LinkedIn, WeChat, and WhatsApp, which connect users to other users where they review and recommend products services while providing opportunities for companies to connect with the users.

And then, we have the e-commerce platforms such as Amazon and Alibaba, where customers can go get reviews from other customers, get recommendations and shop for all their needs.

Then comes omnichannel. The opportunity for firms to interact with users offline and online through different media and channels provides a seamless transition to customers as they move from one touchpoint to the other.

All these new institutions are immersed in the context of their environment - geography, regulation and norms, privacy and security, and their implications for digital marketing.

Then comes the company with its marketing mix elements and marketing analytics interacting with the environment, leading to value creation for the customers and the firm.

Emerging new technologies are constantly changing the environment, the marketing mix elements, and value creation. Marketing strategy in this dynamic, continually evolving environment and marketing capabilities is a roadmap a company needs to have to keep one step ahead of the competition as it serves its customers.

So, here is the digital ecosystem within which today's customers are immersed, becoming aware of products and services, considering and evaluating their options, purchasing, getting satisfied, and sharing their good experiences as new technologies emerge, making it easier for them to do so.

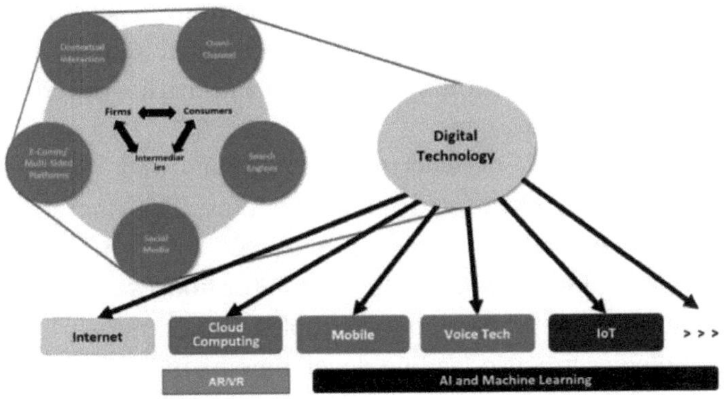

Digital Ecosystem

We are in a progression starting with the internet, cloud computing, mobile technologies, wireless technologies, and voice assistants like Siri, Alexa, and Google Home, Internet of Things (IoT), and anything that might emerge in the future. All are supported by artificial intelligence and machine learning, changing the market landscape.

Let's understand how these digital technologies affect the firm?

Implications

Let's now understand how digital technologies impact the firm. In terms of the marketing mix elements, in terms of analyzing the data generated in the environment and the outcomes for the customers and the firms.

The product concept is undergoing a rapid transformation in the digital age. First, the augmentation of the core product with services is becoming increasingly digital, where the product's core value is increased with value derived from digital enhancements. For example, automobiles with GPS systems, sensor-based self-driving technologies, self-monitoring, and automatic ordering refrigerators, and so on.

Second, the networking of online and mobile technologies is pawning a rental economy. The dominant value of owned products is released through digital networking for rental options. Airbnb for houses and Uber for automobiles are good examples. Such networking technologies are also leading developments in the Internet of Things space. Products are infused with innovative technologies enabling communication with each other and the users.

Third, products and services themselves morph into services, especially in information products, such as software and content such as music, video, and text, with online and mobile technologies playing a key role in delivery and fulfilment. This has provided opportunities to create product lines of various digital and traditional non-digital formats with exciting applications for pricing and marketing. The rise of direct-to-consumer models, such as Mama Earth, BoAT, Wakefit, are all excellent examples.

Product lines of digital services also allow models such as freemium, where the basic version is offered free of charge. The enhanced version is being provided for a fee, as seen in Dropbox cloud storage and streaming online content. The direct-to-consumer models have given rise to subscription pricing models. All these developments also provide opportunities for customizing and personalizing product and service offerings by varying the core product or service and the augmented digital services.

Finally, the explosion of channels, email, search, display, affiliates, referrals, social, and devices, such as laptops, smartphones, smartwatches, Internet of Things, create tremendous opportunities for creative ways to touch and serve customers. Given these technological advancements, firms now have many ways to provide value to customers in terms of value, brand, and relationships and extract the value from customers by increasing their acquisition, retention, and sales, thereby impacting the firm's bottom line positively.

Marketing analytics will play an essential role in this. All the touchpoints of customers in the environment, digital and non-digital, lead to volumes of big data that can inform marketers of how their strategies and tactics are working. Therefore, the role of marketing strategy will be to create a sustainable competitive advantage by selecting the appropriate business model. And of course, as new technologies come into play, this process becomes continuous and dynamic, just as augmented reality and virtual reality are transforming how retailing and home gym services are delivered. So, understanding the framework is key to analyzing and predicting how digital technologies will change marketing as a process and strategy.

In the next chapter, we will examine the marketing process from the viewpoint of first, the customers, and then firms, focusing on highlighting the customer touchpoints and marketing instruments.

CHAPTER IV

Customer Journey

So far, you've read about the concept of digital marketing and the customer's environment. Now, we will focus on the customer journey from general interest to a confirmed purchase by understanding the various stages of the purchase funnel and how the transformation takes a customer from brand awareness to purchasing the product. The purchase funnel analysis will also inform companies on what kinds of marketing messages to send out and at what stages of the journey.

One of the critical concepts that have evolved along with digital marketing is the concept of the Customer Journey. Customer Journey views customers' progression from the state of awareness of a brand, product, or service to its ultimate purchase and beyond as a series of touchpoints where they get information and persuasive messages from the firm or their friends, which impacts the firm their top choice or conversion. In this chapter, I will introduce the concept and a similar concept called Purchase Funnel.

Let's focus on Consumers Purchase Funnel first, i.e., How do consumers become aware of a brand?

The traditional marketing media and instruments that make this happen include print, radio, TV, and word of mouth from friends and acquaintances. In the digital space, this is accomplished by using display ads of all kinds. Banner ads, targeting consumers based on criteria, rich media ads, and native ads all contribute. We will learn more about these in the forthcoming chapters. In addition, digital video word of mouth on social media across both online and mobile devices can be used to create awareness. To make consumers consider the brand for purchase and traditional media, we have displayed ads targeted based on user behaviour online. For example, the kind of websites they are visiting indicating their interest, retargeted ads, and so on.

Online search, email, online reviews, and social media can all help persuade consumers at this stage. These digital media and instruments play a similar role in the intent stage and the purchase stage. After purchase, loyalty is reinforced through email reminders, becoming a fan of the brand on Facebook, Instagram, and traditional means of loyalty programs, direct mail such as catalogues and brochures.

Consumer Purchase Funnel

Consumers are encouraged to become advocates of the brand by providing reviews of the product spreading positive word of mouth on social media, and providing email referrals. As you can see, the marketing media and instruments vary across the different stages of the Purchase Funnel.

Customer Decision Journey

The concept of Customer Decision Journey takes the Purchase Funnel and makes it into a loop. So, consumers become aware of a particular brand or service. The consumer considers an initial set of brands based on brand perceptions and exposure to recent touch points. During this active evaluation stage, they examine the brands they have considered. They may add or subtract brands as they evaluate based on more touchpoints that they come across. Consumers are encouraged to become advocates of the brand by providing reviews of the product spreading positive word of mouth on social media, and providing email referrals. As you can see, the marketing media and instruments vary across the different stages of the Purchase Funnel.

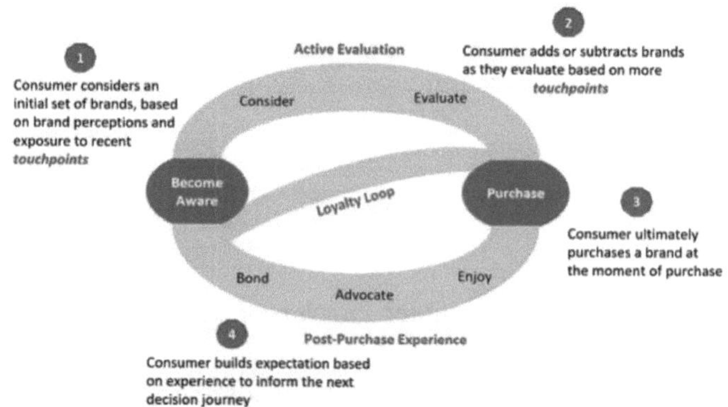

Consumer Decision Journey

Finally, they purchase a brand at the moment of purchase. After purchase, during the post-purchase experience, they enjoy the brand, advocate the brand, and bond with the brand. This provides an expectation based on their experience for the next purchase. If this post-purchase experience has been very positive, they may not even go back to the following evaluation cycle. Instead, they become a loyal consumer and bypass this evaluation stage using this loyalty loop.

It is essential to know that this Purchase Funnel idea can inform us what kinds of marketing messages to send out at different stages of the funnel. Awareness of a brand is accomplished using brand marketing, either on the TV, radio, and traditional media, or using display ads, social media campaigns, etc. This effort is called Brand Advertising. The goal is to create awareness and educate the consumer.

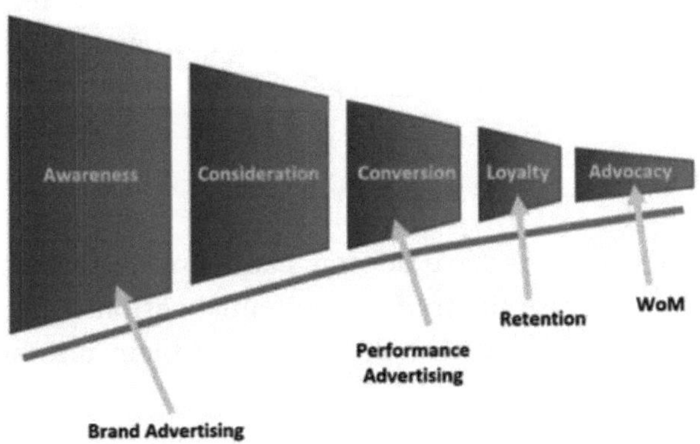

Brand vs Performance Marketing

At the conversion or the purchase stage, the marketing instruments employed are meant to close the sales and make the transformation happen. Online search, email, and retargeted display ads all play a role in the digital space. We call this Performance Marketing, as it is focused on conversion. Then comes Retention and Word of Mouth. Both brand marketing and performance marketing are essential as one starts the journey and the other one closes it.

Inbound and Outbound Marketing

After learning the concept of digital marketing and understanding the purchase funnel related to the customer's journey, let's look at the two different strategies, inbound and outbound marketing. Inbound marketing aims to attract customers who have an inherent interest in the brand. Inbound marketing is also thought to be "pull marketing". On the other hand, outbound marketing aims to push the firm's message to the customer. It is also thought to be "push marketing."

Overview

Digital marketers have several marketing instruments at hand to increase the traffic of potential customers at their website or store so that they can turn them into buying customers.

We classify them broadly into inbound marketing and outbound marketing.

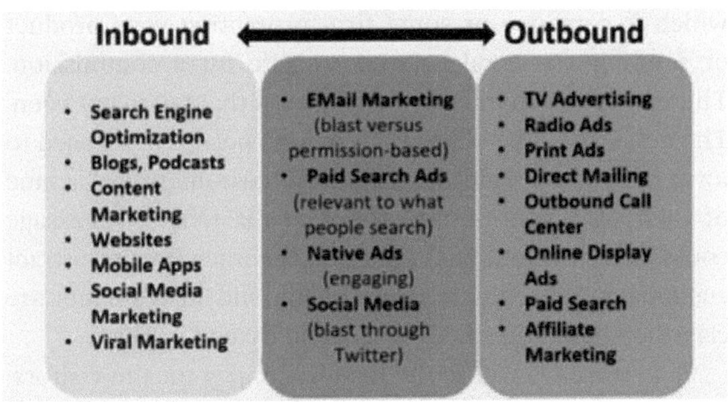

Inbound vs Outbound Marketing

Inbound marketing aims at attracting customers who have an inherent interest in the brand to visit the firm's website more passively. It is pull marketing. Inbound marketing techniques include Search Engine Optimization. You optimize your website so that customers looking for the products you sell can find you easily on search engines. The Blogs and Podcasts made by the firms and picked up by interested buyers can attract them to visit the website.

Similarly, Content Marketing helps create and distribute valuable, relevant, and consistent content to attract the audience of interest to see the firm's website. Having Mobile Apps helps potential customers to connect to the firm when they need to. Social Media Marketing and Viral Marketing leading to solid word of mouth attract potential customers to visit the firm's website.

Outbound marketing is pushing the firm's message to the customers. Intercepting them wherever they are and whatever they are doing. These include TV, Radio and Print, Direct Mailers, Outbound Call Centres, Online

Display Ads, Paid Search Ads, and Affiliate Marketing which is someone or some firm promoting your product or sending a referral to your website for a commission. There are a few marketing instruments that fall in between. The email could be blasted out or sent permission-based to loyal customers. Paid Search where customers may come of their own volition and social media where a message could be blasted out but could also become viral and attract customers. Sometimes, these media and instruments are classified based on paid, owned, and earned media.

Paid media is where the firm has to pay for the visitors, just as in the case of outbound marketing.

Owned media is more similar to inbound marketing and includes entities that the company owns, like its websites, blogs, mobile apps, and its social presence on Facebook, LinkedIn, or Twitter.

Earned media is the word of mouth that the company owns through satisfied leaving positive reviews, the positive press, etc. It includes viral and social media marketing.

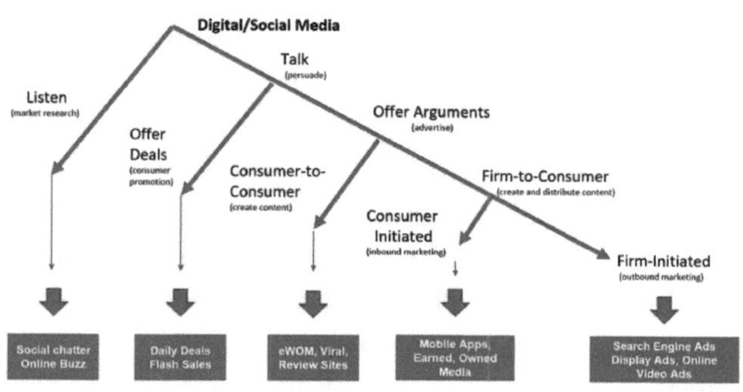

Adapted from Harvard Reading on Digital Marketing

Firms have numerous ways to leverage digital and social media in the digital space. They can do social listening for market research, analyzing the social chatter and online buzz at social media sites. They can provide platforms to customers to share their word of mouth through reviews and help while marketing. They can do inbound marketing, as we have seen before. And finally, they can do outbound marketing.

Ultimately, the firm wants to build its brand awareness and convert customers to its website. All these digital and social media help in that process. A firm that can do these very effectively at the lowest cost will have a sustainable competitive advantage in the market.

CHAPTER V

Platforms and Social Media

In this chapter, you will learn the multi-sided platforms and value creation along with digital marketing design principles, including network effect, pricing, technology, and governance. And in the subsequent chapters, you'll learn the return on investment in social media marketing. Let me introduce the concept of multi-sided platforms, the design and the business principles for platforms. In today's business landscape, everywhere you look, you see platforms. The emergence of platform companies has fundamentally reshaped some traditional industries, such as Airbnb in the lodging industry and Uber in the transportation industry.

But first, what is a platform?

A platform is a business that facilitates value-added interactions between different user groups. The critical components of a platform business include the following.

- First, there should be multiple user groups.
- Second, the platform serves as an intermediary between the user groups.
- Third, value is created in the interactions between participants.

Let's look at example platform in the retailing setting.

Power of Platforms: Network effect

As illustrated, a retailing platform facilitates the interactions between two different users - buyers on the left and sellers on the right. A defining characteristic of the forum is that buyers and sellers interact directly. The platform works as an intermediary rather than a gatekeeper. Thus, a positive feedback group exists between the two user groups. More buyers attract more sellers, and more sellers attract more buyers, known as the network effect.

Let's now look at how a platform is different from a traditional retailer.

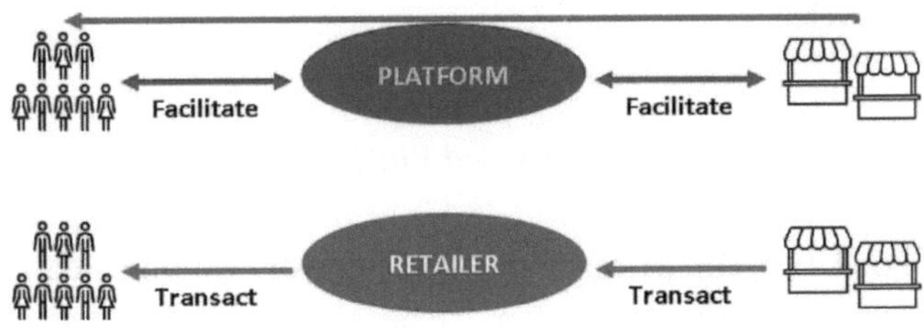

The fundamental difference is that the platform at the top only facilitates the transactions. In contrast, as shown at the bottom, a traditional retailer buys inventory from the merchants and then sells to the consumers. So, from the consumer's perspective, the seller is the platform instead of the merchants. The traditional business model is typically referred to as the pipeline business in contrast to the platform business.

We see examples of platforms in many industries. Amazon and Flipkart in retailing. Uber and Ola in transportation. YouTube, Facebook, TikTok, and Google Ads in the social media and the social network domain.

Furthermore, there are apps and technology platforms and platforms in various markets such as lodging, healthcare, service delivery, and education. And the list goes on.

To understand how the platform business model works. We must start by asking an important question - who are the primary users on the platform.

Two-sided Platforms

For Uber, the primary users are drivers on one side and the riders on the other. For Airbnb, one group of users is the dwelling owners who list their houses and apartment for sharing. Of course, the other end is the travellers who look for a place to stay.

When the platform primarily serves two groups of users, we call them two-sided platforms.

Platforms can also serve more than two groups of users. Take the social media platforms as an example.

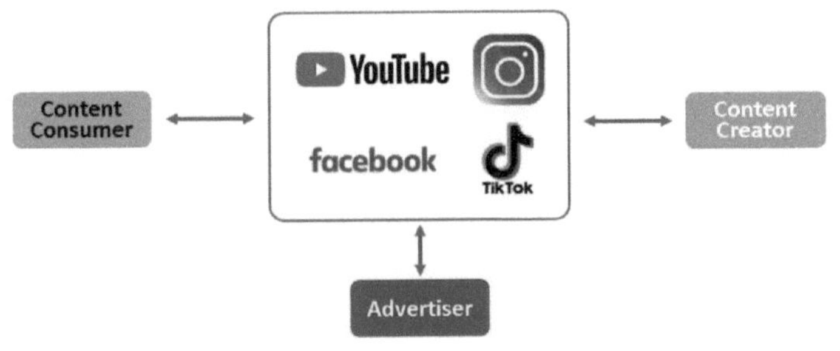

Multi-sided Platforms (MSPs)

One type of user is content consumers who read news and videos on the platforms. Another group of users is content producers who generate and upload the content for others to consume. The third primary type is the advertisers. They pay the platform for the user's attention. By bringing a significant source of revenue, advertisers make up an essential member of the ecosystem on social media platforms. This type of platform is referred to as the multi-sided platform, MSPs.

Why are platforms a solid competitor to pipeline businesses?

The competitive advantages for platforms lay in two aspects.

- First, by getting rid of the gatekeeper. Platforms facilitate direct interactions between consumers and producers, resulting in increased efficiency.
- Second platforms can serve many consumers and producers, simultaneously achieving economies of scale

on both the demand and supply sides. This is a significant advantage. Thanks to the network effects.

CHAPTER VI

Value Creation and Network Effects

This chapter will review the general framework for a platform business. For a platform, the first task is to identify what participants are transacting on it? Second, what value does each user group achieve by joining the forum? The combination of participants and value proposition defines the nature of the core interactions on the platform.

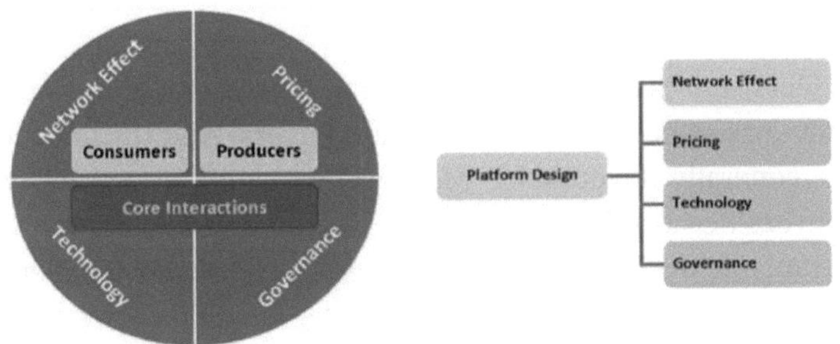

Design Principles

Platforms design considerations revolve around the core interactions; in general, a platform designs its infrastructure based on four reviews.

1. Network effect
2. Pricing
3. Technology, and
4. Governance

Let me give you a broad view on the design considerations related to the network effect using a retail platform as example.

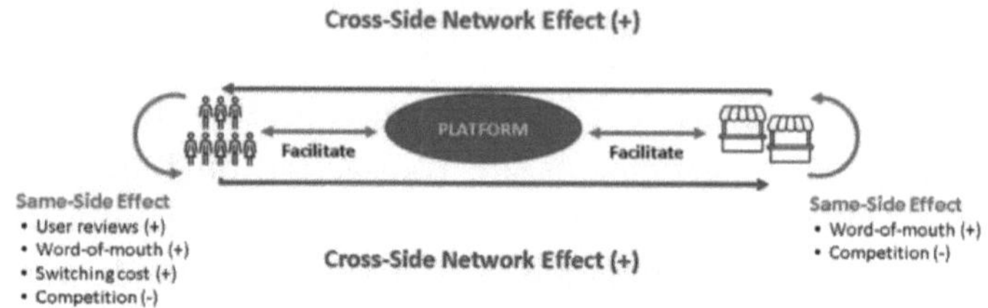

Network Effects

The platform serves two groups of users, buyers, and sellers, on each side of the forum. There is a cross-side network effect between sellers and buyers. And the impact is generally favourable. More sellers will attract more buyers because buyers will have more varieties to choose from. Meanwhile, more buyers will attract more sellers because more buyers create more sales and higher revenue. In addition to the network effect across the sides.

On the buyer side, existing buyers can generate a product to review to benefit future buyers, creating a positive same-side network effect. More buyers could also help develop brand awareness for the platform—another positive same-side impact.

Some platforms can leverage past transaction data to improve their recommendation system. The more users, the better the recommendations. This effect creates a favourable switching cost for users. They would suffer from the worst suggestions if they switched to a platform with fewer users. Of course, not all network effects are positive.

If there is a limited supply, buyers will benefit from fewer buyers instead of more buyers. This would be an example of a negative same-side network effect. The presence of network effects has direct implications on launching a platform.

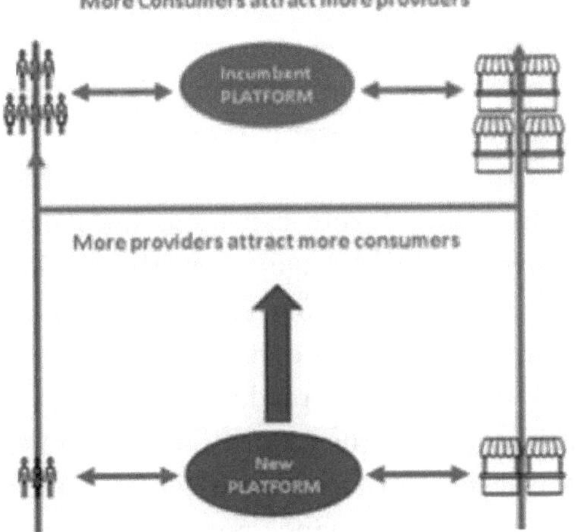

Platform Launch

Compared with incumbent platforms, a new platform will likely have fewer sellers if you are a buyer or both. But order to compete in the seller market, the new platform needs more buyers. To compete in the buyer market, it needs more sellers. The new platform seems to be at a disadvantage on both sides. It is known as the chicken-and-egg conundrum for platform competition.

Several strategies have been proposed and implemented in practice to solve this chicken-and-egg challenge.

- The first strategy is so focused on one side and concentrating the resources quickly reaching a critical mass on this side. This way, the entrance platform can generate competitive advantages, on at least one side, instead of competing high zone on both sides.
- The second strategy follows a similar idea, but instead of focusing on the size of the user group. This emphasis is on the engagement level of a core user group.
- The third strategy is to piggyback on another platform to utilize the existing user base.
- The fourth strategy is known as the bowling pin approach. A new forum can focus on a niche market during the launching stage where the chicken-and-egg problem is relatively more easily overcome. Once the user base has reached a certain level, the platform can then roll out to serve a broader market.
- The fifth strategy is the money-burning strategy. Before the critical mass of buyers and sellers comes, the new platform needs to convince potential buyers that there will be high-quality sellers and convince potential sellers that there will be many buyers.

Media can do intensive advertising or host large-scale promotional events to achieve this goal. The purpose is to signal that they are serious about entering. The signal effect is vital to instil confidence and persuade participants to join the platform.

CHAPTER VII

Platform Design Themes

Platforms operate by focusing on pricing and technology. Pricing includes price sensitivity, cross-side effect, and valuation extraction. Technology is used to attract users, facilitate the interaction between them, and create other matching technologies.

When the strength of one side impacts the growth of the other, these effects can be positive. For example, the more readers a news website has, the more attractive it is to advertisers. The results can also be adverse. For example, the more advertisers a news website shows, the less appealing it is to the potential readers.

The capturing of value from other stakeholders by manipulating the competitive market process to the company's advantage. For example, when consumers' money transfers to merchants, platforms can take a cut and charge a fee. The media are not creating value, and they are extracting it.

Multi-sided Platforms: Pricing and Technology

This chapter will learn the two platform design themes - Pricing and Technology. Platforms typically need to ask two questions-

- How much should I charge on each side?
- Should some users use the platform for free?

Answers to these questions vary depending on the nature of the core interactions on the platform.

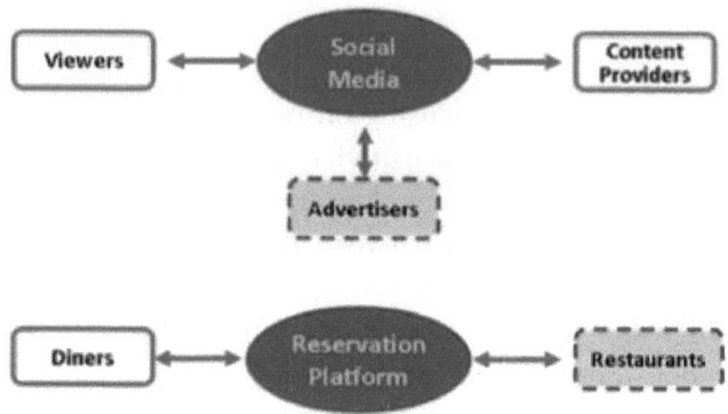

Pricing Examples

For social media platforms, advertisers pay a fee, but consumers and content producers use it for free. For platforms providing online reservation services, for example, booking a table at a restaurant. Restaurants typically need to pay a fee, but consumers use it for free.

Three principles help understand how to design the pricing structure.

- The first is based on participants' price sensitivity. Platforms should charge a higher price when participants have a lower price sensitivity or elasticity level. On the other hand, platforms should charge a lower fee if participants are more price sensitive. Intuitively if one side faces more intense competition from other media, users would be more price sensitive. A lower price should be charged to prevent users from switching to competitors.

- The second principle is based on the cross-side effect. While all user groups derive value from the interactions, the value created would be higher for some groups than others. For example, advertisers value consumers and content producers more than the other way around on a social network platform. Consumers, in general, would prefer fewer ads or no ads. Therefore, platforms charge advertisers, and consumers and content producers pay zero.
- The third principle is based on valuation extraction. It applies to media with money transfers on retailing platforms. For example, money is transferred from consumers to merchants. It is the merchants who extract the monetary gains from the transaction. Therefore, media can take a cut and charge a commission fee to merchants. Consumers use the media for free.

What are some of the popular pricing tactics?

To leverage network effect, platforms sometimes are incentivized to focus on one side of the market and bring the user base to critical mass first. For this reason, platforms commonly give subsidies to some user groups and even allow the participants to use the services for free.

Some platforms allow participants to use the essential services for free to grow the user base. They then charge a fee for premium services. Only participants who have a high platform valuation would need to pay. This combination of free and premium services is known as the freemium model.

Pricing Methods

The third standard pricing method is the subscription model. Instead of charging participants based on usage intensity, the platform uses a membership model and charges a flat fee. One advantage of this model is to encourage the power of engagement because heavy users and light users are paying the same price. The subscription model would be appropriate if platform engagement and the low marginal cost of serving are essential. The following design element for platforms is technology.

Platform technologies fall into three major categories centered around the core interactions.

- The first category is the technologies to attract participants.
- The second category is the technologies to facilitate and support the interactions.
- The third category is the matching technologies.

Due to the size of the user base and the product assortments, the matching technology plays an increasingly important role for many platform businesses.

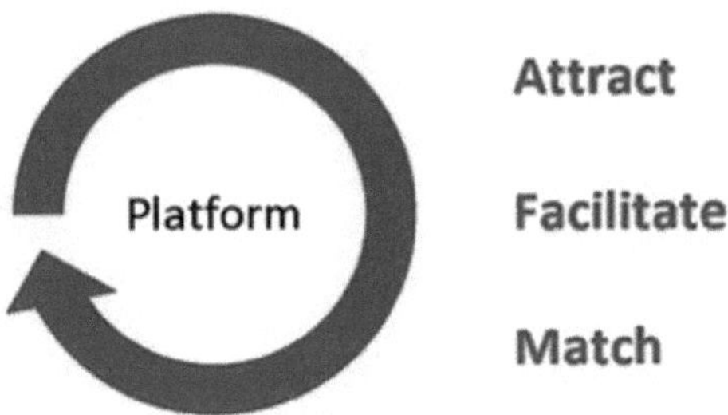

Technology

Examples of matching technologies include recommendation systems that help users discover products or services that match their preferences. Data combined with the technological advances in computer science and data science have led to much development for platform companies to improve matching efficiency.

I'm sure by now you would've understood the importance of pricing and technology when analyzing multi-sided platforms. Platforms must build trust so that users and user groups can pay for services. The media need to carefully incorporate the interrelated operations of control and correction to achieve confidence.

Growth and Governance

Let's now understand another important platform design element - Trust and Governance.

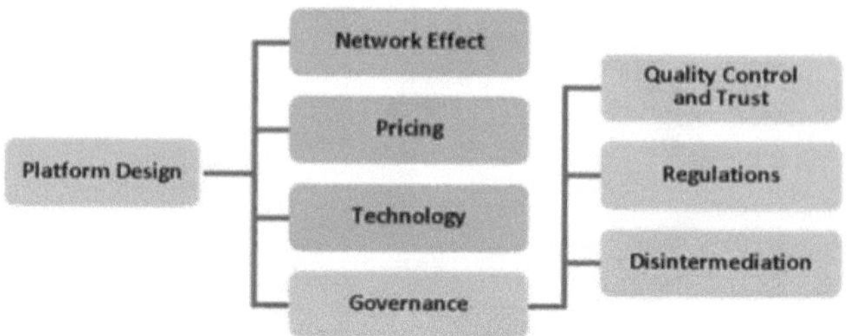

Platform Design

Unlike pipeline businesses, platforms do not directly control the quality of products or services being transferred between participants. Thus, platforms need to carefully incorporate quality control features to build and sustain trust in the ecosystem.

How Do Platforms Build Trust?

User-generated reputation has been named an essential mechanism for platforms to ensure quality control. This user-generated content can reduce uncertainty about quality, and that's how to promote future transactions. The market will filter out products that consistently receive low ratings. User-generated reputation also has downsides.

- First, user ratings and reviews could contain bias and not reflect the actual quality. It is known that users who are extremely satisfied, or unsatisfied or more likely to leave reviews, while those in the middle are less so.
- Second, with user feedback, new products are disadvantaged because they need to compete with those

with existing reputations. This creates a barrier to entry for new products.

- Third, a reputation system is more viable on platforms with repeated transactions.

In certain markets where transactions are infrequent, a reputation would have limited use. Platforms also have the power and the responsibilities to build the trust ecosystem. For this purpose, platforms can implement two interrelated operations.

- Control
- Correction

The control operation means that platforms can use regulations to determine what rules participants should follow. Furthermore, they should also design monitoring systems to control the quality of interactions.

The correction operation speaks to what platforms can do to offset the damage if the current quality control methods fail and conflicts occur. The media need to design policies on punishing behaviours that stray from the regulations.

Let us look at the platform's regulation in more detail.

Platforms use regulations to determine who is allowed to join and what each site is a lot to do.

- The first question is associated with access regulations. Filtering participants can be the first step towards building trust on the platform.
- The second question is associated with behaviour regulations. Platforms need to communicate with participants about what behaviours are allowed and

what behaviours are not.

Depending on their respective regulations, various platforms position themselves somewhere in a spectrum, ranging from entirely open to a completely closed.

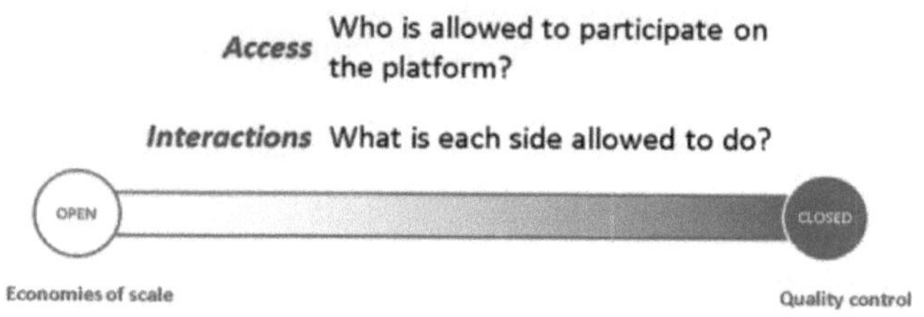

Regulations

Being open, the platform can reach economies of scale more quickly. Being closed, the platform has better quality control and is more likely to build trust faster. In practice, every forum needs to balance the two extremes.

Lastly, it's essential to understand the challenge of this intermediation.

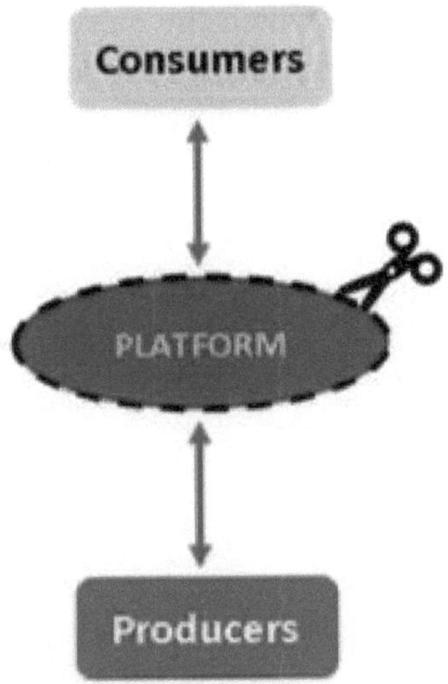

Disintermediation Challenge

When these participants have found a match on the platform, they may be incentivized to go offline and intact directly in the future.

What can platforms do to prevent this?

First, the platform can enhance these regulations on what interactions are allowed on the forum and what information is shared among participants. For example, some venues do not allow direct communication between participants to bypass the platform to transact in the future. Some may ask their participants to sign the agreement and promise not to do future offline transactions.

Another strategy that many platforms are adopting is to provide value-added services to the participants. For example, retailing platforms can provide data analytics services to merchants, which the merchants may not have the capacity to do independently. Providing value can make participants stickier on the forum, which sustains future platform growth.

CHAPTER VIII

Search Engine Marketing

In this chapter, we will take an in-depth exploration of the essential elements of Search Engine Marketing. We will begin with a brief overview of Search Engine Marketing and distinguishing between organic Search (Search Engine Optimisation) and Paid Search. Search Engine Optimisation or SEO, as it is known, will be examined in detail in chapter 11.

Search Engine Marketing is one key strategy in achieving this. Search Engine Marketing is one of the most, if not the most, important customer acquisition activities in digital marketing.

Why is search engine marketing important?

Search Engine Marketing is a form of Internet marketing that seeks to promote websites by increasing their visibility in search engine result pages (SERPs) through search engine optimization, paid placement, contextual advertising, and paid inclusion.

> "*Webopedia defines search engines as; "Programs that search documents for specified keywords and return a list of the documents where the keywords were found." Whilst it has a generic meaning, the term is often used to describe some of the prevalent web search engines.*"

It is worth noting that some practitioners use the term SEM to refer only to paid search activity. In this course, the broader definition of SEM is used, including both Paid and Organic Search (SEO).

Organic Search or Search Engine Optimisation (SEO)

SEO involves getting the best rank or search position in the organic listings on a search engine results page (SERP), following a search on specific keywords or key phrases. These listings sit below the top PPC or sponsored links (which are revenue sources for the search engines).

Paid Search

In the broadest sense, paid search ads appear when a potential customer is searching for an answer or a product. Most paid search is charged on a pay-per-click (PPC) basis. The terms paid search and PPC are sometimes used interchangeably. PPC involves paying when an ad is clicked on, with the advertising triggered by keyword search results on search engines. Within Google, for example, the top PPC text ads (up to 4) are listed above organic search results and are denoted as Ads. (As per the example below.)

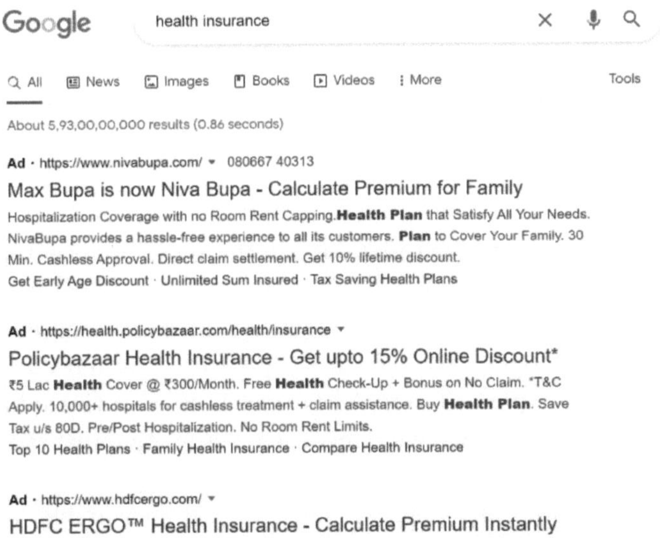

This screenshot shows the search results for "Health Insurance", with paid adverts in the top, followed by organic search results

Other text ads can be located at the bottom of the page. Some paid search on the Google Display network is charged on a cost-per-impression (CPM) (when the ad appears); or cost-per-action (CPA) basis (when an ad leads to a sale or other conversion), the focus here will be on the most common approach - paid search using pay-per-click (PPC). A recent global study found that, within the search category, paid search equated to just over 5% of website traffic, with organic providing the rest. (These figures did not include mobile, where it is anticipated that paid will likely be a more significant contributor than these figures suggest.)

Types Of Paid Search Advertising

Outlined below are the most popular forms of Paid Search / PPC advertising.

1. Expanded Text Ads

These keyword-based text ads are the most popular type of PPC ad. They can be ahead of or below the organic listings, and they must be identified as ads. Since early 2017 in Google, text ads can only be created and edited using the Expanded Text Ad Format Link icon (including two headlines of 30 characters each, description text space 80 characters, and an option to use a display URL). Text ads have the advantage of being highly measurable and can be tracked and managed with relative ease. They are relatively straightforward to set up, but they are also highly competitive and require some experience and expertise to leverage their unlimited opportunity.

2. Ad Extensions, e.g., Site Link Extensions, Location and Call Extensions

Ad extensions can include extra information added to a text ad, such as a phone number, call button, site links to critical parts of the website, or business location address. One or more extensions can be used. Many extensions are only available on the search network, and there is no fee to set up extensions. Still, fees apply when interacting with the extension (e.g., calling business, getting directions).

This Google Ads tutorial (rb.gy/ingvpv) from Google describes how ad extensions can help your ad stand out from the crowd and demonstrates choosing the right ad extension based on your business goals.

3. Product Listing Ads / Google Shopping Ads

Product Listing Ads (PLAs) or Google Shopping ads are CPAs (cost-per-action) ads where you only pay for conversions. These ads have more product information such as an image, price, and merchant name. They are tailored around products and product categories (instead of keywords). Ads can appear at the top of search results or the upper right-hand side of the results page.

The Google Shopping platform (owned by Google) is powered by Google Ads and the Google Merchant Centre, incorporating tax and shipping rules. Google determines ad placement on Google Shopping, determined by factors including ad feed, bidding, monitoring, and optimization. Visitors can be taken to a specific site (click on-site) or to the relevant Google Shopping comparison page (click on product category).

4. Local Inventory Ads

These ads feature business locations and are designed to direct web users to call or visit the business. These ads are charged on a standard CPC (same as PPC).

Local Inventory Ads (LIAs) can work in concert with standard PLAs. For example, when a shopper is within a (designated) proximity to the store and searches on their mobile, they can be presented with both channel options in their PLA. Clicking on 'In Store' would direct consumers to the local storefront; they would be directed to the website if they click on the product title. The LIA option can be set to show only when people search within a designated distance from the store.

Introduction To the Google Ads Structure

A key aspect in achieving success in Google Ads is establishing a correct structure for your Google AdWords. Good design enables control over how the ads are triggered and where and when they are seen. This can result in a better-quality score (Google's rating of a site) and support efforts more effectively. WordStream summarizes the steps needed to build a paid search account structure.

Let's consider the critical structural elements.

1. Ad Campaigns:

Ideally, a campaign is developed for each business goal or product category. It is likely an advertiser will have a few Ad Campaigns. Budgets are set at this level, as is the location targeting.

2. Ad Groups:

These are more specific than Ad Campaigns. While there is no prescribed number within an Ad Campaign, too many Ad Groups will stretch a budget very thinly. Different Ad Groups are formed to address different keywords.

3. Keywords:

These are critical in determining how an ad is triggered. Generally, there are no more than 5-20 keywords per Ad

Group. When a search query is matched with a keyword or key phrase, the keyword(s) trigger the text ads and direct people to a relevant landing page. Each keyword has a maximum CPC, match type Link icon, and a quality score. It is essential to research keywords and to establish a keyword strategy. Negative keywords are also important to consider. They help prevent an ad from being shown to the wrong audience and save unnecessary costs through inappropriate clicks.

4. Ad Text:

The actual text will appear when the ad is triggered. A suggested number is around 2-3 ads per Ad Group, directing to the same landing page. Different ads can be A/ B tested over time to evaluate the most successful one.

Steps In Setting Up A Google Ads Campaign

Step 1:Define your Marketing Goals

As with any marketing campaign, understanding the marketing goals is essential. This is critical in determining how a campaign should be set up.

Step 2:Choose the Campaign Type and Settings

Deciding where to show the ads and what format to use is critical. The Google Search Network uses a text ad shown on Google search and Google partner sites when people are searching for similar products and services. These people are searching for products/services related to the ad offer (by keywords, key phrases).

The Google Display Network is where ads are placed on websites, mobile apps, and YouTube and are matched to relate to the content being viewed. Display ads format can be text, video, images, or rich media. Beyond text ads, display ads often require higher creativity, as website visitors need to be persuaded to click into the site. These ads generally have a lower CTR and are considered for their brand-building benefit. Display ads are not 'search ads' (as viewers are not actively searching), but they operate using a PPC model. Alternatively, users can maximize exposure (largest audience) by combining the two networks with a Search Network with Display Select option.

This is managed similarly to a search network option (setting a budget, using keywords, creating ads, and setting bids).

What Settings to Customise the Ad Campaign?

Settings on the campaign subtype help advertisers choose the level of flexibility and control they want. For example, a 'Standard' subtype does not provide much flexibility for the advertiser to control. Alternatively, an 'All feature' setting enables daily manipulation and customization of campaign aspects such as scheduling days, times, frequencies, and targeting ads to particular locations or websites. Google Display Network allows advertisers to choose related sites and other placements. Advertisers can choose specific sites, pages, demographic groups (based on age, language), etc.

Step 3: Selecting Geographic Locations

Locational settings can be used in Google Ads.

Advertisers can be as specific as a local area (within a 5 KM business radius) or can nominate cities, regions, and states in a country. Budget can become an issue if geographic locations become very broad.

Location settings happen at a campaign level, so overall, these need to be established for the whole campaign.

Step 4: Setting a Bid

Choosing the right bid strategy. Generally, higher bids and highly relevant keywords result in higher ad ranks. However, advertisers can adopt one of two key bid strategies within CPC bidding:

1. Manual CPC bidding strategy (advertiser sets their own CPC bids at an Ad group or keyword level)
2. Automated 'maximize clicks' bid strategy (AdWords automatically sets recommendations working within the daily budget).

Step 5: Setting a Daily Budget

How much the advertiser is willing to spend on the campaign per day. Google recommends starting with a smaller daily budget and re-evaluating after a few weeks. Google provides Ads tutorials for each of these steps.

Step 6: *Organising Your Account: Setting up Ad Groups*

There is no definitive structure for organizing an Ads campaign. It will depend on several factors, starting with your marketing goals. At a campaign level, some of the more significant decisions are made. Each campaign should address a different marketing goal or product category, as we have briefly outlined. Campaigns are where budgets sit, and decisions are made regarding timing and location settings. It is also helpful if campaigns match the broad categories within a website.

Step 7: *Choosing the Right Keywords*

Keywords are words or phrases that trigger ads to match a potential customer's search. They are critical to ad success. Consider the following tips:

- Think like a customer – what would the customer search for?
- General keywords will reach more people – but may get potentially fewer conversions
- Organize keywords by Ad Groups or themes
- Select specific keywords for each Ad Group (5-20 keywords per Ad Group)
- Keywords or keyphrases (of 2-3 keywords) are often relatively, more effective
- Use negative keywords – to ensure any irrelevant searchers are removed
- Another helpful strategy in choosing the right keywords is to use Keyword Planner (Google's keyword research tool) or similar.

Step 8:Establishing Match Criteria for Keywords

A keyword match criterion is selected, indicating how specific or general the keyword matches can be.

Step 9: Writing an Effective Ad

Practice makes perfect when writing an effective ad. Text ads writing tips include:

Have a Strong headline

- Ensure the (two) headline sections make sense when read as one or as two sections
- The headline should highlight the unique aspect of the business
- The headline should be directly relevant to the keywords being searched
- A strong headline will also be appealing to the searcher

Display URL

- This should ink to a strong landing page that connects with the ad and where action can be taken.
- Description text should:
- Highlight key benefits of product or service

- Include a unique selling proposition (USP)
- Use a call-to-action – what do we want the viewer to do?
- Ideally include any key sale items or discounts, exclusives, promotions
- Include some keywords

Ad Extensions

Consider useful ad extensions, e.g., for mobile customers - location and call extensions could be beneficial. Google Ads is quite a vast platform. There are many different types of ads. So, most people think of it as a search ad because you think of Google and Ads. So those are the ads that come up at the top of your Google search, the basic text ads. And then, you can also have banner display ads, which are the images you see on websites that pop up. There are different display ads as well, so you can have prospecting, depending on the strategy. So that's sourcing new customers. You can also have remarketing, which means people have been to your website, had a little browse, left without buying anything. Then you serve them ads to remind them to come back and buy your product.

There are so many different ways to do it, and you have to think about, what is your goal, and what is your strategy? And once you set it up, continually check and optimize. Different industries have different plans and regulations. So, you need to keep your consumers top of mind and think about what would make them click on this ad and entice them to buy my product over others advertising in the same space.

When you're first starting to use Google Ads, I would say, play around. Start small with your budgets. Test-and-learn is the best way. It doesn't have to be perfect the first time. You set up a few variations, set up a few strategies, different targeting methods, different ads, and set them live. And that's the only way you're going to learn, and it will be different for every business, whether it's in the same industry or not, it's other brands, different customers.

So, the only way to get it efficient is to improve continually, and just set it live, so that would be my advice. And make sure you're looking at the data and results regularly to ensure that you're not losing money or something might be broken. Some things can quickly go wrong in the digital world, so you need to keep an eye on it regularly and not just set it up and let it go.

CHAPTER IX

Search ROI

In the previous chapter, you looked at Search Engine Marketing, Search Engine Optimization, and the "cost per click" that consumers and advertisers pay. In this chapter, you will learn the concepts of Return on Investment (ROI), Click-Through Rate (CTR), and Transaction Conversion Rate (TCR). I will help you understand the differences between the ROI - Return on Investment and ROA - Return on Ads.

You will now learn how to determine the return on investment on search engine marketing. This is important because, as a digital marketer, you have several options to invest your money to get the maximum traffic to your website. The ROI metric allows you to compare search engines, search campaigns, and other display and social media marketing options.

Search Engine	Media Spend	Total Impressions	Total # Clicks	Cost per Click (CPC)	# of Bookings	CTR	TCR	Prob Booking
Bing	$123,000	1,806,306	72,894	$1.69	788	4.04%	1.08%	0.0004362
Google	$346,000	3,845,660	192,107	$1.80	1,954	5.00%	1.02%	0.0005081
MSN	$18000	170,120	10,807	$1.67	145	6.35%	1.34%	0.0008523
Yandex	$72,340	18,080,435	60,901	$1.19	379	0.34%	0.62%	0.0000210
Baidu	$143,200	17,062,488	119,325	$1.20	294	0.70%	0.25%	0.0000172
Yahoo	$47,000	933,345	45,595	$1.03	670	4.89%	1.47%	0.0007178
Total	$749,540	41,898,354	501,629	$1.49	4,230	1.20%	0.84%	0.0001010

Search Campaigns of a Hospitality Chain

We see on the exhibit above the results of running paid search campaigns across many different search engines for a luxury hotel chain. Each row gives you the details of the campaign. As you see in the last row, the hotel chain has spent about $750,000 on these campaigns.

Let's look at the first row - the result for the campaign on the search engine Bing.

The firm has spent 123,000 at Bing and has obtained 1.8 million impressions. They had about 73,000 clicks leading to nearly 788 bookings at the luxury hotel chain's website. The abbreviation CTR stands for Click Through Rate. And the term TCR stands for Transaction Conversion Rate or simply Conversion Rate.

The last column is the probability of a conversion given an impression. So, at Bing, an Ad impression of this luxury hotel chain has a 0.04% chance of converting.

So, let's examine these metrics closely.

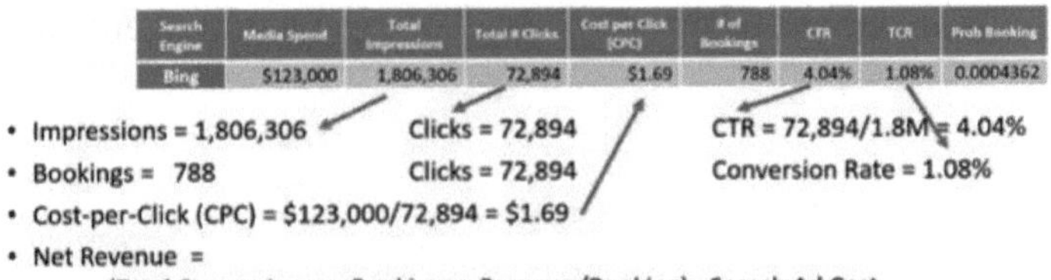

Search Engine	Media Spend	Total Impressions	Total # Clicks	Cost per Click (CPC)	# of Bookings	CTR	TCR	Prob Booking
Bing	$123,000	1,806,306	72,894	$1.69	788	4.04%	1.08%	0.0004362

Metrics

So, if you look at the exhibit above, you'll understand that I have reproduced the numbers for Bing. We have 1.8

million impressions leading to about 73,000 clicks. This allows us to calculate the Click Through Rate as 4.04%. Bookings were; 788 out of the clicks of 73,000, leading to a Conversion Rate of 1.08%. The Cost-per-Click is the amount spent divided by the number of clicks. This gives us $1.69.

So, what is the net revenue?

We determine the total revenue received and subtract the full amount invested in Ads.

Let's assume that from each booking, we get thousand dollars. So, applying it to this case, net revenue from search is determined to be; conversions times revenue per booking, minus search Ad cost, which gives us $665,000.

So, what is the return on Ad Dollar? That is the return for each dollar spent at Bing.

We divide 665,000 by 123,000, which gives us 540%. So, every dollar invested in Bing search gets you $5.40 in net revenue.

Now, we can compare the ROA across all search engines.

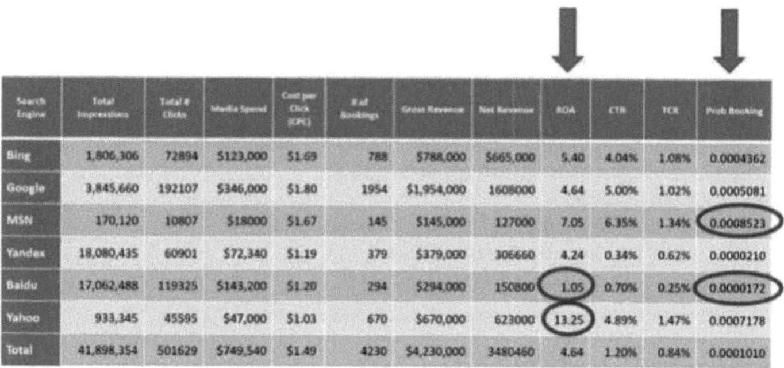

Search Engine	Total Impressions	Total # Clicks	Media Spend	Cost per Click (CPC)	# of Bookings	Gross Revenue	Net Revenue	ROA	CTR	TCR	Prob Booking
Bing	1,806,306	72894	$123,000	$1.69	788	$788,000	$665,000	5.40	4.04%	1.08%	0.0004362
Google	3,845,660	192107	$346,000	$1.80	1954	$1,954,000	1608000	4.64	5.00%	1.02%	0.0005081
MSN	170,120	10807	$18000	$1.67	145	$145,000	127000	7.05	6.35%	1.34%	0.0008523
Yandex	18,080,435	60901	$72,340	$1.19	379	$379,000	306660	4.24	0.34%	0.62%	0.0000210
Baidu	17,062,488	119325	$143,200	$1.20	294	$294,000	150800	1.05	0.70%	0.25%	0.0000172
Yahoo	933,345	45595	$47,000	$1.03	670	$670,000	623000	13.25	4.89%	1.47%	0.0007178
Total	41,898,354	501629	$749,540	$1.49	4230	$4,230,000	3480460	4.64	1.20%	0.84%	0.0001010

Yahoo provides the highest return, while Baidu is the least. We can also compare the probability of booking across all search engines. MSN has the highest chance of getting a conversion, while Baidu is the lowest for an impression.

Comments

These return on Ad Dollars or return on investment figures; were done at the search engine level, but you can do the same, at the keyword level, within a specific search engine.

So, you can compare the return on Ad Dollars of different keywords. The automated bidding algorithms take these ROA figures into account to bid across keywords. We can do similar ROA/ROI calculations across; search, email, display ads, etc. We need to consider these ROIs for allocating marketing budgets across these marketing instruments.

So, this chapter gave you an idea of how well your search campaign is doing across search engines.

CHAPTER X

Inbound Marketing

This chapter covers an essential practice in digital marketing – 'Inbound Marketing. Inbound marketing, as a concept, has been around since about 2006 but has gained great popularity in more recent years. We will explore what is meant by 'Inbound Marketing' and examine its growth in recent years. The characteristics and role of inbound marketing will also be discussed and compared to outbound marketing.

The growth of inbound marketing is not surprising, given some of the issues we have addressed within this course. Consider the impact of consumer empowerment, including ad-blocking, coupled with the role of the organic search in generating web traffic. These combined factors mean that businesses need to find ways to attract people to their brands and add value in the process. The enhanced power of consumers and their rising cynicism has meant that businesses need to consider different approaches in generating leads, nurturing these leads, and building personalized and valued relationships over the longer term.

In the forthcoming chapters, we will explore SEO or organic search and take a close look at SEO keyword and key phrase optimization and on-page optimization.

What is Inbound Marketing?

Given the increasing popularity of 'Inbound Marketing', let's consider two definitions from Chaffey & Smith and HubSpot.

"Where the consumer is proactive in seeking out information for their needs and interactions with brands, attracted through content, search and social media marketing.
(Chaffey and Smith)"

"Inbound marketing is focused on attracting customers through relevant and helpful content and adding value at every stage in your customer's buying journey. With inbound marketing, potential customers find you through channels like blogs, search engines, and social media.
(HubSpot)"

These definitions highlight that publishing quality content is core to inbound marketing and attracts visits through SEO and social media. Marketing isn't the same as it used to be. These days you can't just buy a commercial or big newspaper ad and expect customers to flock to you. Now, with the Internet, marketing is completely changed. Small and mid-sized businesses have access to millions of people, but marketing must be done differently. Thankfully inbound marketing makes it easier for small businesses to be hugely successful by using the Internet to market.

Meet Rajeev. He left his job last year to start his own small business. He loves being his boss and has hired a few employees. Rajeev's business grew through word-of-mouth and then lots of networking. Now Rajeev is ready to start developing the company into his dream business. He tried to increase his networking, but handshake marketing has already produced all of its customers. Rajeev can only attend so many meetings, and there aren't limitless networking opportunities in his town. He's also reached out to all of his friends and contacts, so they have given him all the business and introductions that they can. Expanding his reach through his current customers only helped a little bit. Because everybody is on the Internet, Rajeev decided to try Internet marketing; he didn't know where to start. He knew he needed a website, so he got his nephew to build one for him. The business didn't increase. Rajeev heard that people find websites through search engines in their browsers and that links like votes determined rankings. If a site has more links, it ranks higher and more people find it.

He hired another small firm to try and rank his website higher so more people would find him and his business would grow. But people didn't see him, and his company didn't succeed. Then one of Rajeev's friends told him about inbound marketing; she said to him that instead of trying to rank high in search engines or running costly ads in newspapers and television, inbound marketing was a way of delivering great value to people to start building relationships. They would find him and come to his business. Not only would prospects come to his business, but they would also be his ideal prospects as they had seen and chosen him. She described the difference between traditional marketing and inbound marketing. She said that traditional marketing was like hunting elephants in the forest when they had all moved to the savanna. No matter how hard you hunted or what techniques you used, finding an elephant in the woods was almost impossible. Inbound marketing would be like finding out that the elephants preferred the savanna. Further research showed that the place they liked best was the watering hole. Then they would find a spot around the watering hole that was far enough away from the animals not to disturb them. The elephants would show up and stay for quite a long time, allowing for plenty of pictures.

Rajeev realized that by providing great value, understanding what his prospects wanted, giving it to them, and not trying to sell to them immediately, they would begin to find him. Not only would they see him, but it would also let him stay in touch giving him opportunities to help them solve future problems. He found a firm that could help him define his goals and set up an inbound marketing system based on social media and a blog and began to put his newfound knowledge to work. Rajeev's business began to grow slowly at first, but as time went on, it grew faster and faster, and his pool of prospects grew and grew.

Rajeev had to add a few more employees to keep up with the growth. He found inbound marketing to be much more enjoyable than traditional marketing. Even better, he found it to be much less expensive.

By now, you may have already identified differences between inbound and outbound marketing, including inbound is not interruptive and is permission-based, inbound relies on having relevant and helpful content, and inbound communication is two-way. It involves prospects coming to the business rather than actively pursuing opportunities.

Types of inbound marketing activity

These largely reflect SEO and different forms of content marketing; however, email marketing and referrals (via word of mouth; news/media/PR) are also included. The majority of referrals are now done via social media platforms.

Types of Inbound Marketing

The Role of Inbound Marketing Across the Buying Cycle

Inbound marketing has been readily associated with the early stages of the buying cycle. However, in reality, inbound marketing can support all stages of a buyer's journey.

There have been changes in both buyer behaviour and business activity that have likely contributed to this broad remit for inbound marketing. Let's briefly consider the buying cycle itself. It has been argued that digital has changed the buying cycle fundamentally. Customer empowerment has created a buyer cycle that the buyer now drives.

Mckinsey states that:

> "*Today's buyers are more quickly moving through the pre-purchase phases and extending loyalty and advocacy phases for much longer, so long as their experience, positive or negative, is polarizing enough for sentiment.*"

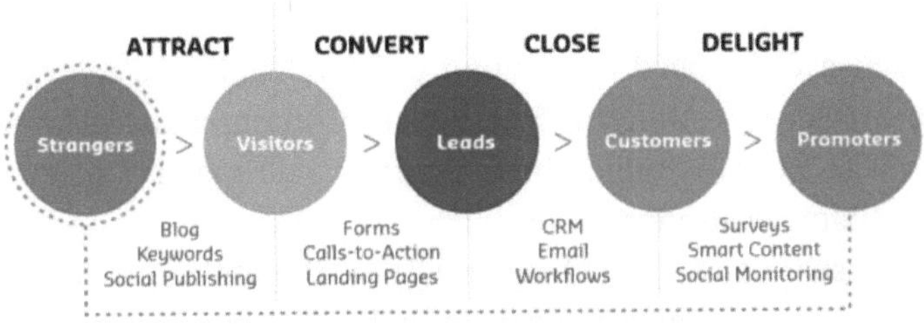

Buyer Cycle

A helpful framework by HubSpot captures the buyer's cycle in four states (or business actions) needed to move 'strangers' to 'promoters'. It describes critical inbound tools and digital processes across the different activities.

CHAPTER XI

Content Marketing

The Content Marketing Institute offers a clear definition of content marketing:

> *"Content marketing is a strategic marketing approach focused on creating and distributing valuable, relevant and consistent content to attract and retain a clearly defined audience - and, ultimately, to drive profitable customer action."*

It is worth reflecting on this definition. We have already discussed the need for content to be valuable and relevant to attract a well-defined audience. Content must also be consistent (to build brand trust), ultimately driving profitable customer action.

Barker et al. (2017) suggests that the ability to deliver against this definition consistently has become increasingly challenging, given the multitude of channels to consider and that search engine marketing favours certain content such as blogs, tweets, and white papers in search results.

We will explore three popular content marketing elements in detail: Mobile Apps and Gamification

- Video Marketing
- Blogs

Mobile Apps and Gamification

Mobile Applications (Apps) are computer software applications designed for small wireless devices. As mobile device use continues to grow, so does the market potential for apps.

Apps provide benefits for both consumers and businesses. According to Forbes and Vividus they-

- Enable customers to readily access the brand's content and utility (function)
- Increase a brand's visibility by its presence on mobile devices
- Provide opportunities to add-value to the customer relationship
- Reduce some business costs associated with SMS messages, phone queries etc
- Strengthen customer engagement and therefore help to nurture loyalty
- Enable the business to control the consumer information (as an owned asset)

A consumer's micro-moments are those numerous decision-making moments when a consumer wants their needs met in real-time and with relevance. Unsurprisingly, mobile apps can play an integral role in meeting consumers' needs in their micro-moments. Think with Google research looks at how people discover and engage with apps and what brands can do.

For an app to strengthen customer engagement, it must be perceived as valuable and appealing to engage with. One popular strategy employed in app development (and across some social media platforms) is gamification. The use of game mechanisms, such as contests and prizes to a non-game activity, builds interactivity and, therefore, brand engagement. Often gamification is added to an existing concept to provide fun, incentive, and motivation.

Video Marketing

Video content is an essential tool for marketers. It is reportedly used by around 87% of online marketers. A WordStream survey of professional marketers and SMEs found that over three-quarters of those who used video marketing felt it directly impacted their business.

Video marketing offers three main advantages:

1. **It is suited to the creation of strong viewer engagement:** the visual medium provides opportunity to humanise a communication, tell stories and attract through appealing visual content.
2. **It taps into a large audience:** Consider these two WordStream statistics: YouTube has over a billion users, almost one-third of all Internet users.
3. **Video format supports product promotion:** Promoting a product's features and benefits; or providing explicit details on product usage is very well supported by video content.

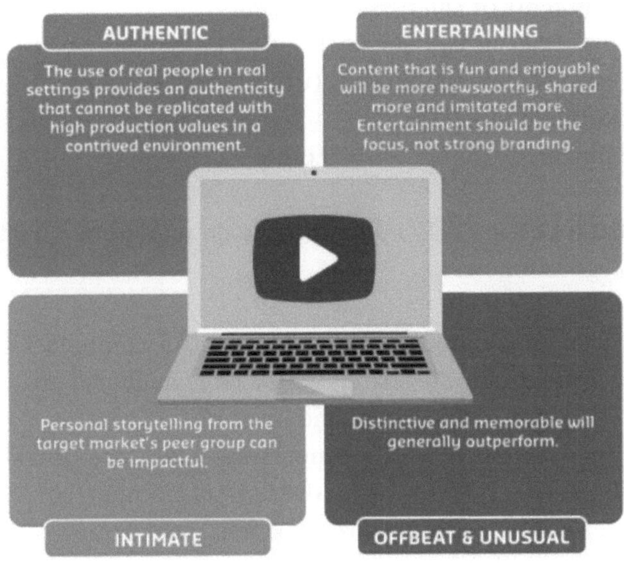

Key Elements of an Appealing Video Content

Blogs

A blog can be defined as a:

> *"Frequent, chronological publication of personal thoughts and Web links."*

Barker et al (2017) define the six characteristics that distinguish blogs from other types of social media as:

- Publishable (cheap and easy to publish)
- Findable (can be found through search engines)
- Social (blogs can facilitate connections – links to other comments or can invite comments)
- Viral (can spread quickly)
- Able to be syndicated (using RSS, readers can be notified of updates)
- Linkable (can link to each other)

Barker et al (2017) define the main marketing benefits of blogs as follows:

- Blogs enable deep, rich, and insightful comments and information to be shared with a large audience through text, video, audio, links, and images.
- Blogs support word-of-mouth as they are linkable, findable, and stimulate discussion, rather than just creating a general buzz (which many other social platforms do).
- Blogs enable accessible and rich customer feedback and response on various topics or ideas.

Tracking customer feedback and sentiment is essential and can be achieved via social listening software or free tools to measure key metrics in Blogger and Google Analytics.

Scalable Content Marketing and Content Automation

Once an organization has created strong branded content based on good customer insights, it needs a clear strategy to distribute this content. Using communications channels that are appropriate to the target market is essential. Additionally, to fully leverage the potential impact of branded content, marketers should consider strategies to scale content for maximum distribution. Scalability relates to the use of content across a whole range of media.

Consider traditional media. Traditional media had limited scalability as it was people-intensive and different distribution required more people.

However, content scalability is much more possible now due to digital platforms.

> "*Content is near infinitely scalable on the Internet. The Internet was built to scale content in seconds.*
> ***(Tom Foremski)***"

A brief blog by Lush Content Agency introduces three tips for scalable content marketing.

- Keep it focused on business objectives
- See the longevity in content
- Cut costs and effort by creating brand partnerships through content

wo approaches that can be used to scale content distribution are content automation and amplification. Let's examine these approaches.

Content Automation

Digital platforms enable the automation of content. Consider the following example from Content Marketing Institute.

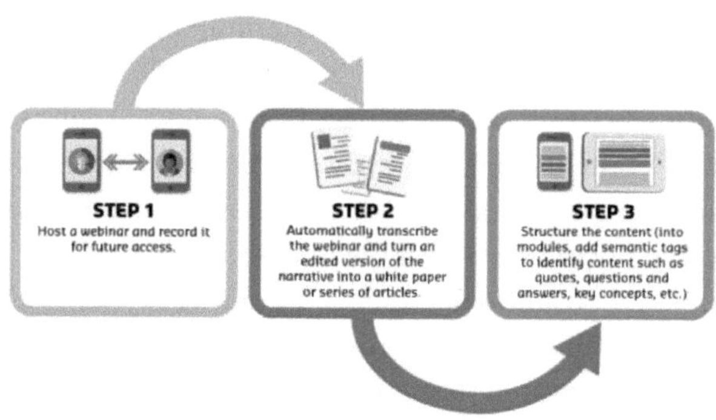

Use automation of this content to scale the distribution. For example:

- Extract the questions and answers (based on tags) and turn them into blog posts.
- Compile the blog posts into a digest post of the top "X" things you need to know.
- Extract key quotes and tweet them.

- Take the same questions, post them to Facebook, and start a conversation.

Scalable Content Marketing and Amplification

According to Content Marketing Institute content amplification is:

> "*A a multichannel approach that uses paid, owned and earned media to promote and distribute content.*"

Content amplification is the overarching concept that describes many different strategies and approaches that brands employ to get their content more broadly into the market. Fundamentally, amplification is the distribution strategy for your content. Using paid digital ads, organic search, or engaging influencers on social media are all examples of amplification strategies. It can be paid or unpaid (organic) amplification.

The need to amplify has been driven by:

- The proliferation of content developed (e.g., 3 million blogs posted per day)
- The decline in organic search (particularly on social platforms)

In the study published by WordStream there are four tips to achieving amplification.

Tip 1: *Only amplify really good content*

Tip 2: *Leverage the power of influencer marketing*

Tip 3: *Use 'Super Remarketing' (remarketing to users with similar characteristics to those that visited your site)*

Tip 4: *Maximise opportunities in niche communities*

Future Trends in Content Marketing

Four content marketing key trends identified are outlined below.

1. Continued Focus on Content Marketing

Organizations continue to focus on content marketing and report higher levels of success in the succeeding year. Greater focus on content means businesses will invest more in content marketers, building teams that continually develop valuable, unique, and personalized content for customers. These trends will result in content marketing getting a higher proportion of the marketing budget and more focus in an organization.

2. Role of (paid) Amplification

The proliferation of content means that growth in active content amplification is required. It is suggested that the importance of paid amplification will continue to rise.

Purchasing influencer marketing is likely to be a vital component of this.

> "*Look for influencer marketing to shift a bit from partnering with content creators and distributors to flat-out purchasing them.*
> ***(Content Marketing Institute)***"

Cielo

3. Role of Visual/Video Content

The role of visual and video content continues to grow in influence in the Internet experience, creating a deeper engagement.

4. Personalisation

With increasing competition in content marketing, it is predicted that personalized content recommendations will become prevalent. Research from Forrester Consulting demonstrates a trend towards customized marketing. Marketing automation will enable much of this personalization, allowing customers to have a unique experience based on their needs.

CHAPTER XII

Search Engine Optimisation (SEO)

Chapter 8 identified that Search Engine Optimisation (SEO) involves getting the best rank or search position in the organic listings on a search engine results page (SERP), following a search on specific keywords or key phrases. SEO is one of the strategies within the broader concept of Inbound Marketing.

SEO continues to evolve and can require significant resources and expertise because of the frequent algorithm changes by search engines. The constant need to monitor and update SEO activity may result in marketers questioning its usefulness.

Evidence suggests that SEO remains an essential component of an Inbound Marketing strategy. The role of the Internet in the purchasing cycle and evaluation of website traffic sources shows that around one-third of web visits come from organic search. A HubSpot survey found that 61% of marketers say improving SEO and growing their organic presence is their top inbound marketing priority Optimising keywords and key phrases is an important SEO activity.

Let's explore the basis of keywords, key phrases, and on-page optimization.

The role of search engines is to match the enquirer's search keywords with the most relevant content. Therefore, marketers need to make their keywords/ keyphrases highly relevant.

Keyword Or Key Phrase

Quora defines a keyword as a single word used in a search. Looking for shoes online, your keyword search might be 'shoes', 'Nike', or 'Adidas', for example.

A key phrase is a combination of keywords.

The search could be 'Nike shoes' or 'school shoes'.

Chaffey distinguishes between the two, arguing that a focus on key phrases is more important as Google places more relevance on a phrase match on a page. While the focus here is on SEO, it should be noted that these considerations on keyword and critical phrase optimization are also essential for paid search.

How does a marketer optimise the keywords/ key phrases that they should adopt?

There are four broad approaches to keyword/key phrase optimisation.

1. Demand Analysis

This involves examining the demand/popularity of the search term, its relevance to the product or service, the user intent, and the competition. Chaffey and Smith (2017) suggest that demand analysis would likely include a combination of:

- Using tools such as Google Keyword Planner and Google Trends will provide estimates of keyword and critical phrase popularity.
- Market knowledge
- Examining competitors' sites

- Using web analytics to look at the key phrases used by the visitors that have come to the site already
- Examine the internal website search tool (searches within site)

2. Performance Analysis

This second approach to keyword/critical phrase optimization involves assessing how well the company is performing for the phrases. Different methods including: can undertake this

- The use of tracking tools (rank-checking tools, such as Google Search Console Analytics, and others
- The volume referred from search
- The click quality (conversion rates, bounce rates)
- Outcomes (sales, leads)
- Costs and Profitability

3. Gap Analysis

This involves identifying and listing the key phrases currently used and then prioritizing them in importance or value to the business. How do these then compare with the words that prospective customers use? Market Maven describes how this leads to the steps required to bridge this gap.

4. Set goals and select key phrases

Identify specific key phrases that a business needs to have visibility and presence. There will be strategic considerations on ensuring particular vital words will provide visibility for your brand. This may relate to the most profitable or core products to the business and the positioning.

Factors Influencing Search Engine Ranking

Many factors can influence ranking (e.g., Google cites over 200 ranking factors), and these factors can change. Moz states that Google changes its search algorithm 500-600 times each year.

Changes to the search algorithm can result in changes in rankings achieved and SEO.

Chaffey and Smith (2017) identify common factors that influence search engine rankings, and we will look at two key factors: on-page optimization and external linking.

1. On-page optimisation

A search engine will determine the critical phrase relevance (i.e., the website's potential relevance to the search query) based on factors including:

- Frequency of times, the key phrase appears on the page.
- If the key phrase is in headings or the anchor text of hyperlinks
- Text mark-up, e.g., bold
- The proximity of the phrase to the start of the document, gap between keywords

- Alternative image text (which is hidden text associated with graphical images on a website). While users will not see this text, search engines can contribute to relevance.

Document metadata (which is the hidden text used to describe individual web pages). Certain metadata can be useful for SEO. The HTML <title> tag is important as search engines give significant relevance weighting the key phrases in it. The description metadata, HTML <head> section is also useful.

Business Perspective

Organic search is an essential part of the digital marketing mix, and it's necessary to get it right from the outset with the site structure. As we know, Google changes its algorithm on an ongoing basis regarding what will be optimized and get you up the list. The one thing that hasn't changed is whether it be subdomains or the URL structure and the importance of those, and making sure you've got those keywords in the site structure.

With all the content growth, both written and video content, the content must be authentic, accurate, and integrated into the site. A lot of content sits alongside a blog or something like that, which might get traffic to the site.

If it's integrated with the product where it's adding value and forms part of the site, it's much more effective in getting the transactions and the results. So, it's essential that content forms part of the whole strategy and that you're asking for that as part of the feedback process. When you've shipped a product, you're following up; you're getting the feedback and getting that content and closing that loop through, and making sure you're driving that content strategy.

Digital marketing is a vital channel. And it's essential to understand how it fits into the board or marketing mix. For some organizations, it can be, in fact, the whole marketing budget, and for others, it's a minor part of it, depending on your audience and what your product is. But it is essential to understand it. The thing is, it's constantly changing, and it's a constant challenge to keep up to date with the news channels that are emerging or even the existing channels, how they are changing. If you're a smaller organization, you need to pick a few of those channels and do them well. It's impossible to be an expert in all of them. Larger organizations have more resources and bigger budgets; again, you still can't do them all, but you can have experts specializing in certain areas.

Often, we see paid, and organic search teamed together, sometimes with content. Sometimes a range sitting alongside social, occasionally social sits alongside customer service. So, it can depend on your organizational structure, but you must be constantly aware of what's emerging by having social listening. You'll see where your customers are and what they're saying, and that can often help you prioritize.

The critical thing with digital marketing is that it's all very measurable, so you can test and learn and constantly evolve to ensure you're getting the best out of your resources. Digital marketing, or marketing broadly, it's still essential that you're very clear on the strategy and that that's right from the outset. And that fits in with the whole business strategy; it's not just an isolated marketing strategy. You must understand your target market very clearly and understand the channels and reach them. Now that has changed. There are a lot more channels available now. And with that has become a lot more data. That can be a pro and a con because often you can't see the data for the trees, but it's essential to be able to understand what that data means and how to use it, how to interpret it, and how to present that back to the business in a way that can add value.

CHAPTER XIII

Multi-Channel and Attribution

This chapter covers the importance of holistic marketing efforts with multi-channel, mobile marketing, and multi-touch attribution. Mobile represents 65% of digital media time. Mobile gives users 24/7 access and combines physical and digital world connectivity. Most companies now have mobile-optimized websites giving them complete access to consumers. Let me help you understand Mobile Marketing, Proximity Marketing, and Multi-devices Mobile Marketing.

Why mobile marketing?

The potential of digital space for marketing took a paradigm shift when mobile technology ushered in the era of any time anywhere ubiquitous connectivity. Let's examine the power and flexibility of mobile marketing.

Let's first focus on the basics of mobile marketing.

There has been a steady increase in users‘ time on mobile devices over the years. Devices such as laptops, smartphones, tablets, and smartwatches, of which mobile now represents 65% of the digital media time, so much so that desktop has become a "secondary touchpoint" for many users. Mobile spending has increased significantly across Display, Search, Short, and Multimedia Message Services.

So, what is so unique about mobile marketing, and where do its power and flexibility come from?

- First, it allows 24/7 tracking of a user to provide interceptions at the right time.
- Second, it seamlessly combines the physical and digital worlds, using connectivity leading to an explosion in omnichannel possibilities.
- Finally, it is personal and allows precision targeting. You don't have to worry about who the person is using the mobile device, unlike a desktop.

Combining all the above three points, you have a powerful way to connect with individual consumers anytime, anywhere across physical and digital spaces.

Mobile marketing technologies include Mobile Websites and Mobile Apps, Short and Multimedia Message Services, QR codes, mobile wallets, Proximity optimized tools such as Augmented reality, Geo-targeting, and Geo-conquesting and smartwatches.

Mobile Websites can be very different from the online websites of the same companies. Why is this?

It is because of the footprint of available space. The websites need to be optimized for customers "on the go" to get the information they want, given the limitations of smaller screens, colour limitations, need for quick download and navigation, etc. Mobile Websites have to be optimized for wireless access, flash/javascript, etc. While most companies have a mobile-optimized website, having a mobile app is a different question. Mobile apps can be faster, more interactive, and can take advantage of other phone features, like mobile banking, and be more engaging. 80% of the time spent on mobile is on mobile apps, but they're not inexpensive. They require content updates for quality, need platform approval, Android or Apple app stores, and customers need to install it on their phone.

While this is possible for apps that consumers use a lot, many downloaded apps are never used, and they are deleted over some time by users. SMS it's like a text message, and MMS allows images to be sent. Customers need to opt in so that companies can send them these messages.

Companies can set up Geo-fences. A Geo-fence is a virtual perimeter around a mall or a store using GPS technology that indicates that a user with a smartphone has entered the frame. They can use technology to Geo-target customers based on some criteria - Demographic, or whether they have the company's app and so on and push messages and coupons. They can also set up Geofence around the competitor's location and Geo-conquest the customers.

Let's now continue focusing on the other capabilities of mobile marketing.

Mobile and Proximity Marketing

By now, you must be well aware of geofences and how companies use GPS technology to target smartphones using customers with specific ads. Let me now shift the focus on advanced strategies, and features companies can use for mobile marketing and how Quick Response (QR) codes can be a form of marketing.

What you have read so far is only a part of the capabilities of mobile marketing. The more advanced capabilities are fast emerging. A typical application is a quick response or QR code. These give Mel the physical world with the digital world by providing access to different kinds of information - product info, website links, prize campaigns, address, maps, etc. These are extremely popular now, not only in Japan that it was created in 1994, but all over the world.

Another technology is proximity marketing. These are accomplished by using beacon technology as a consumer gets closer to a display. Beacons can identify the user by ID'ing their phones and sending personalized content. Bluetooth is another technology that will be more familiar to all. These enable localized wireless distribution of advertising content associated with a particular place or location. The Bluetooth server sends content to the discovered mobile devices as you get closer.

Applications such as mobile social networks and augmented reality work on this technology.

Augmented reality, AR as it is commonly called is an interactive experience of a real-world environment where the objects that reside in the real world are enhanced by computer-generated perceptual information, sometimes across multiple sensory modalities, including visual and auditory senses. New technologies are emerging that can provide even smell, touch, and sensory experiences like touching a piece of cloth or smelling flowers. This is an exciting area for novel applications.

Uses of proximity marketing include media distribution at concerts, information, gaming, social applications, retail check-ins, payment gateways, and local advertising.

Proximity marketing isn't one single technology; it can be implemented using several methods. And it's not limited to smartphone usage. Modern laptops that are GPS enabled can also be targeted through some proximity technologies.

- **NFC** – The phone's location may be determined by near-field communications (NFC) enabled on the phone connecting to an RFID chip on a product or media. NFC is the technology deployed for Apple Pay and other payment technologies but doesn't have to be limited to payments. Museums and monuments, for instance, can install NFC devices to provide tour information. Retail outlets can deploy NFC on shelves for product information. There's a ton of marketing opportunity with NFC technology.

- **Geofencing–** As you move with your phone, your cellular connection is managed between towers. Text message marketing systems can utilize your location to push text messages to only those devices within a specific region. This is known as SMS Geofencing. It's not a precise technology, but it can be helpful to ensure your message is only sent to the target audience you need at the time you want.
- **Bluetooth** – Retail locations can utilize beacons that can connect to your smartphone. Typically, a mobile application enables the technology and requests permission. You can push content through Bluetooth, serve local websites from WiFi, utilize the beacon as an Internet access point, act as a Captive portal, offer interactive services, and operate with no Internet connection.
- **RFID** – Various technologies use radio waves to identify objects or people. RFID works by storing a serial number in the device identifying an item or person. This information is embedded on a microchip that is attached to an antenna. This is called an RFID tag. The chip transmits the ID information to a reader.
- **Proximity ID** – These are proximity cards or contactless ID cards. These cards use an embedded antenna to communicate with a remote receiver within a few inches. Proximity cards are read-only devices mainly

used as security cards for door access. These cards can hold a limited amount of information.

Companies who wish to develop these platforms utilize mobile applications tied, with permission, to the mobile device's geographic location. When the mobile app gets within a specific geographic area, Bluetooth or NFC technology can pinpoint their location where messages can be triggered.

As you read in this chapter, mobile technologies have a significant potential for marketing applications, and this is an emerging frontier. It's pretty well-known that consumers use multiple devices to do their shopping. They may watch TV and use a tablet simultaneously to shop, then switch to a desktop to complete their purchases. They may be traveling by train and using their smartphone at the same time to surf and then come home and switch to a tablet or desktop. This leads to device fragmentation, which means marketers need to understand the consumer usage of devices across time in the day and across the purchase funnel.

The usage and switching between devices provide valuable insights into customers' stage. Customers typically start on a mobile device and end their journey on the desktop. Knowing this can help online retailers identify critical moments in the customer journey as to when they switch, i.e., when their conversion probability more than doubles—serving the customer by providing a seamless transition for across device shopping - like the basket remaining the same when customer switch can help customers go smoother through the journey and lead to conversions.

Mobile is a valuable device for online retailers worth investing in despite the low direct conversion. The lesson here is that we need to take a holistic view of the devices and channels, as consumers today use multiple channels and devices, and we cannot view any channel or device in isolation.

CHAPTER XIV

Social Media Marketing

It is common for people to have an opinion on the role and benefits of social media, given its pervasive use. This chapter explores the strategic role of social media marketing (SMM) within a broader digital marketing perspective.

What is Social Media Marketing and what are the benefits?

A good overview of Social Media Marketing is provided by Barker et al., 2017.

Social Media Marketing:

- Involves gaining website traffic or attention through social media sites.
- It relies on the production of engaging content that seeks to both attract attention and encourage earned media through the sharing of that content by third parties (via their social networks)
- It supports a greater level of trust for an organization, as their messages are being shared by third parties (other users) rather than being distributed as promotional messages from the organization. They effectively use earned media to build awareness and trust rather than paid media.

Dispelling Myths

The pace of social media adoption and its different (earned media) model have generated several myths around SMM. Four common myths are discussed and dispelled below.

Myth 1:*Social Media is Just a Fad*

With almost 4.5 billion people active on social media (2021), and growth of social media use of 21%, the use of social media is not a fad. Platforms such as Facebook enable users to: Connect, Create, Enjoy, Learn, Transact and Give. As of 2021, Facebook is the largest social media platform globally, with 2.85 billion monthly active users worldwide, and 75% of them spend 20 minutes or more on Facebook every day.

Myth 2:*Social Media is Just for the Young*

While younger age groups remain the highest social media users, the growth of use in older demographics has been substantial. Pew Research (examining social media use across age groups, shows social media proportional use for 50-64yr olds has increased to 50%, and for 65+yr olds, it has grown to around 35%.

Myth 3: *There is No Return on SMM*

The Annual Social Media Marketing Industry Reports provide insights into SMM. The 2019 Report found 92% of marketers stated that SMM was critical to their business. The same industry report (2015) cited that 70% of companies with more than 5yrs SMM use felt that SMM had helped improve sales. Buffer Social surveyed 1,700 marketers and reported that companies that invest in social media ads are more than twice as likely to say social media marketing is "very effective" for their business.

Well-known SMM campaigns such as The ALS Ice Bucket Challenge demonstrate exceptional returns when strategically suited and well-executed campaigns.

In analyzing the potential benefits of SMM, the desired return will not always be sales or profit – in this instance; it was a catalyst for social good and non-profit fundraising. Barker et al. (2017) cites the top three benefits of SMM as increased exposure, increased traffic, and fan loyalty development.

Myth 4:Social Media is Free

While using social media platforms can be free, there are still significant costs involved in social media marketing.

These include both personnel time (in-house and third-party) and technology resources. Content needs to be high quality to attract attention in busy SM environments. Development time is required to produce good content that will generate the desired benefits. Social media platforms also need to be managed and monitored on an ongoing basis.

What Makes Social Media Marketing Different?

Barker et al. (2017) identify three key differences between social and traditional marketing.

1. Organisations contribute to, not control SMM

The dynamic of earned media underpins the success of social media marketing. We know from earlier discussions that made media involves media generated by third parties (not by the organization). Organizations need to relinquish some control and recognize that they can be contributors in helping to shape/influence engagement about their brand, but they do not have complete control. This earned media model differs from the corporate power of traditional media.

2. Trust building is approached differently on social platforms

Organizations need to build trust through authentic and honest contributions within the social sphere. SMM supports ongoing customer interaction, so dishonest brands can 'get caught out and ultimately suffer brand reputation damage.

It is also worth noting that the ability to build trust on social platforms may be eroding. A study on behalf of the Chartered Institute of Marketing found that 30% of consumers had little or no confidence in the brand information they see on Facebook.

3. SMM requires different creative and technological skills

SMM blends vital marketing creativity with technology. As technology evolves, the creative options for organizations continue to grow.

Barker et al. (2017) suggest that you must consider how good creative content will work on social platforms and how they will integrate into broader digital and fully integrated marketing campaigns.

Key Social Media Marketing Concepts

I will introduce the concepts of Exposure; Engagement; Influence; Impact, and Advocacy and then examine the permission versus interruption social media marketing.

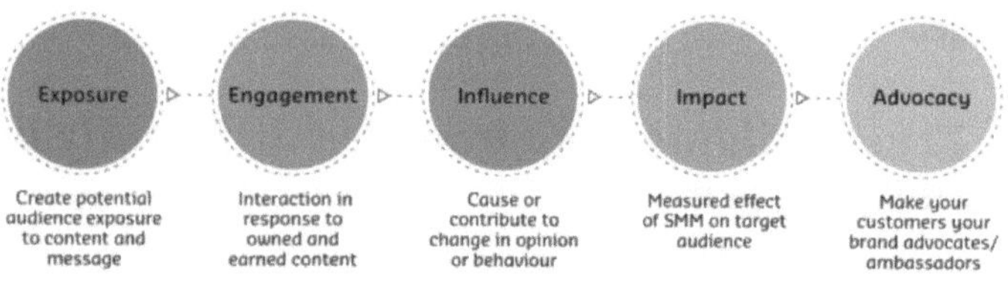

Exposure

Exposure is not a new concept. In its broadest sense, exposure refers to the opportunity to see/hear a piece of content on any channel. Social media enables earned media to be leveraged, thereby facilitating high brand exposure opportunities.

Engagement

Engagement is a widely used term in digital marketing, with a range of varied definitions. Let's consider two valuable reports.

A business starting in social media engagement may initially adopt a passive approach, including searching for their own and competitor brands, listening, and providing a simple response to people engaged with their brand.

Barker et al. (2017) recommend that a more proactive engagement strategy would involve creating and growing social profiles, connecting with influencers, starting conversations, and actively participating in existing discussions. Proactive engagement can be more powerful, but brands should first understand their customers and their type of engagement on social platforms.

Influence

Influence relates to the ability to affect attitudes and behaviour. Influencers can play a critical factor in SMM due to the growth and perceived trustworthiness of recommendations and their amplification in earned media. A Nielsen study found that earned media is the most trusted form of advertising, mainly from friends or family.

Understanding how to leverage influence in a marketing campaign is essential. Social media influencers can be engaged to help connect a brand to its target audience. However, choosing the right brand influencers is critical. Influencers have to have a solid contextual brand fit and be connected to the target audience. Influencers connect with their audience and their audience (or networks), making them very powerful if the fit is right. A good influencer will build brand awareness and help increase brand traffic and drive sales.

Influencers can range from mega-celebrities to more everyday consumers who are perceived to have expertise/ credibility and a trusted relationship with the target audience. Identifying key influencers can involve participating in conversations on social media platforms, joining relevant communities, or conducting a more formal search that provides influencers' scores.

Impact

Impact refers to how a social media marketing activity affects business results. Does it help to achieve the business/marketing objectives? Gullans (2016) argues that the fundamental problem with social media marketing is the lack of a common denominator to measure its return on investment (ROI). Various measurements are used, including numbers of fans, followers, retweets, shares, level of referral traffic from other platforms, and number of sales via social referrals.

Gullans also suggests five steps in measuring SMM effectiveness, including identifying KPIs to understand what success looks like, aligning SM goals with business objectives, using Google Analytics to track conversions, assigning monetary value to the goals, and benchmarking against competitors.

Advocacy

A brand advocate is a customer who speaks favourably about a product or service. They believe in the product/service and, in effect, will help to advertise it through word-of-mouth. Advocacy can have a significant impact on social media.

CHAPTER XV

Permission Vs Interruptive

Permission Marketing is when consumers consent to be marketed to, and it relies on attention being earned from the audience.

In effect, permission marketing is organic social marketing. Examples include: opting into an email newsletter, following a Twitter account, or signing up for text message alerts.

In many respects, permission marketing has created more significant equity in the marketplace. Previously, influential brands with big budgets could have dominated through interruptive advertising. The requirements for permission marketing campaigns ensure that the drive is highly engaging, supported by authenticity, empathy, respect for customers' time, and a vital human element.

Interruption Marketing reflects the traditional marketing model when marketers control and can interrupt (push) marketing messages at their target market. In a social media sense, interruption marketing relates to social advertising, such as sponsored or recommended posts. These posts may be based on:

- Interest targeting (activities, skills)
- Behavioural targeting (devices, keywords on post)
- Customer targeting (specific individuals)
- Lookalike targeting (similar audience)

Nelson (2021) cites figures from the Social Media Examiner's Social Media Industry Report 2018 regarding proposed advertising on social media. The industry survey found that two-thirds (67%) of businesses plan on increasing their use of Facebook advertisements in the coming year, and 53% plan on more investment in Instagram advertising in the same period. Successful SMM campaigns generally employ some mix of both permission and interruption marketing, as social platforms (such as Facebook) use extensive advertising.

Ten Laws of Social Media Marketing

According to Susan Gunelius, author of 10 Laws of Social Media Marketing, leveraging the power of social media can elevate your audience and customer base, but getting started without any previous experience or insight can be challenging..

The ten laws will help build a foundation that will serve you well.

1. The law of listening.

Social media success requires more listening and less talking. Only then can you create content and spark conversations that add value to your audience's lives.

2. The law of focus.

It's better to specialize than to be a jack of all trades. A highly-focused social media strategy has a better chance for success.

3. The law of quality.

Quality trumps quantity. It's better to have 1,000 connections sharing and talking about your content than 10,000 connections who disappear after connecting with you.

4. The law of patience.

Social media success doesn't happen overnight. While it's possible to catch lightning in a bottle, it's more likely you'll need to commit to the long haul to achieve results.

5. The law of compounding.

If you publish great content and work to build your online audience, they'll share it with their audiences. Others sharing and discussing your content opens new entry points for search engines to find it. Those entry points could grow to thousands of ways for people to see you.

6. The law of influence.

Spend time finding the influencers in your market. Connect and work to build relationships with them. If you get on their radar, they might share your content with their followers.

7. The law of value.

You must add value to the conversation. People stop listening if you spend all your social media time promoting your business. Focus less on conversions and more on creating content and developing relationships.

8. The law of acknowledgment.

You wouldn't ignore someone who reaches out to you in person, so don't ignore them online. Building relationships is essential, so always acknowledge anyone who reaches out to you.

9. The law of accessibility.

Don't publish your content and then disappear. Be available. Consistently publish content and participate in conversations.

10. The law of reciprocity.

You can't expect others to share your content if you don't do the same for them. A portion of your time on social media should be focused on content published by others.

Reviewing some of the most successful recent social media campaigns is another good way to understand the SMM key principles at work.

CHAPTER XVI

Social Listening

Social listening is the ongoing process of tracking online conversations. It is highly beneficial to understand the tone of online communities and identify target audiences' preferred social platforms and activities.

Barker et al. (2017) suggest five stages of social listening. A brand should listen to:

- Conversations about their brand: identifying issues and opportunities will help prepare when joining the discussion.
- Conversations about their competitors: knowing what customers and competitors say about the competition help identify potentially competitive areas for a brand.
- Conversations about the industry or category: identifying industry issues people are most concerned with or interested in will benefit.
- The tone of the community: understanding the norms and unwritten rules of community interaction; and the keywords, jargon, slang, or acronyms used can all be beneficial to a brand's social participation.
- Different social platforms: understanding that other social channels have different audiences with their own interests, behaviours and characteristics. A brand needs to identify the critical platform(s) used by its target market.

Two essential concepts apply equally to social analytics.

1. **A/B Testing or Split Testing** involves the comparison of two versions (e.g., of a webpage or app) to examine the specific impact of each variable and which performs best.
2. **Selection of Relevant Metrics** that are appropriate to the campaign objectives is essential. A range of quantitative social media metrics is listed below, adapted from Barker et al. (2017).

Exposure

- Page visits
- Visitors, unique visitors
- Visits per channel (source)
- Reach – total follower/audience count
- Opportunity-to-see
- OPM (cost per thousand exposures)

Engagement

- Repeat visits
- Time spent on site
- Total interactions on post/page
- Likes, shares, comments
- Click-throughs
- Number of followers/friends
- Total audience from shares
- Interaction with profile
- Use of hashtags

Influence

- Links
- Associations with brand attributes
- Purchase considerations
- Likelihood to recommend

Impact

- New subscribers
- Number of referrals to website
- Number of content downloads
- Number of app downloads
- Abandoned shopping carts
- Number of sales leads
- Conversion rate
- Sales/repeat sales
- Purchase frequency
- Cost savings

Advocacy

- Online ratings
- Ratio mentions to recommendations
- Number of brand fans/advocates

Three Levels of Social Media Listening

Social media listening provides companies with actionable insights in real-time. But not all companies have the same capabilities to implement social media listening. Let me present a framework for understanding how social media listening evolves as the organization becomes more sophisticated. This framework can help you structure your organization's social media listening activities for maximum impact.

Social media listening is powerful, yet the data are messy and not necessarily easy to analyze. In addition, social media listening data can be analyzed using both qualitative and quantitative approaches. We can think about social media listening as a process with three levels.

First Stage: *Observation and Monitoring*

Observation and monitoring involve systematically setting up processes to observe consumer conversations about brands. These processes range from very simple and inexpensive. For example, they set up alerts for notifications when the brand is mentioned on a platform to elaborate and expensive—for instance, developing communities explicitly designed to learn about consumer experiences. Social monitoring provides insights to the firm about consumer choice and consumption behaviour through the consumer's voice. In addition, by monitoring social media platforms, firms can keep on top of consumer issues or problems that might arise. Finally, engaging in social media monitoring builds researchers' and marketers' intuition about the brand and consumer behaviour and forms a foundation for sophisticated mining capabilities.

On the downside, social monitoring focuses primarily on what happened and tends to be descriptive. Therefore, social monitoring may raise more questions than it addresses, and it is not well suited to situations with specific research questions.

Further, the insights may be anecdotal, such as a series of tweets about a product feature. These observations do not necessarily reveal statistically-significant behaviours to sway critical business decisions. However, observations and monitoring alerts often serve as excellent examples of quantitative analytics in reports.

Second Stage: *Data Mining*

At this stage, the unstructured set of social listening data is analyzed. One way data scientists study information is by using text analysis. For example, companies can measure the sentiment of brand-related and competitor-related comments. In addition, data can be combined and analyzed with other data sources, such as website analytics or purchase behaviour. Combining data sets allows for a much deeper dive into specific business questions. Implementing data mining requires more sophisticated analytic capabilities relative to observation and monitoring.

Third Stage: *Predictive Analytics*

At the most sophisticated level of social media listening, firms use social media data not just to explain consumer behaviour but to predict consumer behaviour. Companies use observed social patterns, including interactions, sharing, and search behaviour to forecast sales or indicate when a trend will pop. Then retailers can use these predictions to adjust their forecasts and buying decisions. Predicting consumer behaviour can also allow firms to offer a more personalized approach to the consumption experience. Of course, predictive analytics are not 100% accurate. No amount of data will equal a crystal ball with a clear view of the future. In addition, predictive modeling requires highly-trained analysts.

Three levels, as mentioned above, of social media listening can be applied within an organization. These levels range from descriptive observation and monitoring to data mining techniques on social media data to uncover insights to sophisticated analytic methods for prediction. In the next chapter, we overview some of the standard methods used to analyze social media marketing data.

Understanding where you are in terms of the stages above will help you take better advantage of social media listening and develop your firm's capabilities to advance to the next level.

Tools and Techniques

Let me provide some background information about the process and approaches used in analyzing social media data. The methodologies and tools underlying these approaches are constantly evolving. Therefore, my goal is to provide you with a general framework for social media analytics.

Big Data Sources and the Collection of Data

Social media data come from many online sources, including microblogs, blogs, forums, consumer review sites, and other social platforms. There are a variety of approaches used to collect this data. Google Alerts and RSS feed subscriptions can track brand and competitive mentions for smaller companies with limited resources. With increasing resources, several apps, companies, and agencies offer data collection services and provide dashboards for ongoing monitoring of social media activity at a variety of levels of sophistication.

While social media data on their own can be informative, the ability to inform marketing decision-making through data mining and prediction is enhanced when social data are combined with other sources. Dubois and Haumant (2017) suggest that three types of data inform marketing decisions:

1. **Social Data**, such as online conversations, can reveal consumer preferences and sentiment about brands
2. **Search Data**, which is linked to personal interests
3. **Site Data**, which can reflect behavioural outcomes, including purchase

Combining these three data sources will maximize your ability to understand relationships within the data and make predictions about future trends.

Analytic Methods for Social Media Data

Gandomi and Haider (2014) suggest that there are two basic approaches to the analysis of social media data. Content-based analytics include extracting information from online text, audio, video, and images collected from consumer-generated social media sources such as blogs, microblogs, question-and-answer sites such as Quora, and other social media platforms. Analytic techniques such as natural language processing, machine learning, and computational linguistics are used to derive meaning from these data sources. They range from basic descriptive information to deriving sentiment and opinions on specific topics. Content-based approaches provide insights into consumer attitudes and beliefs.

Structure-based analytics are used to map social networks and understand how information flows within these networks. These methods can identify communities and the influencers within communities. For example, you could use network analysis of Twitter data to identify communities and influencers in the Internet of Things (IoT) sector. These findings inform firm-level strategy and tactical decisions such as choosing social media influencers and identifying sales leads.

To summarize, to take advantage of the opportunities offered by social media marketing data, firms need to implement processes to collect data from a wide variety of sources and combine these data with other data sources, including data related to online search and website visits transactions.

Once data is collected, there are two general approaches for drawing meaning.

- Content-based analytics focus on understanding what consumers are saying about the brand, competitive brands, and the purchase and consumption process more generally.
- Structure-based analytics use patterns of information exchange to identify communities and the influencers within those communities.

CHAPTER XVII

Assessing Social Media ROI

Social media marketing managers need to assess the positive outcomes of their investments in social media marketing, i.e., the social media Return on Investment, or ROI. Understanding ROI is the holy grail of social media marketing. However, attributing consumer awareness, knowledge, or behaviour changes to a specific social media investment can be challenging.

In this chapter, I will help you explore how to assess the ROI of social media efforts. Considering social media ROI starts with the brand's business goals, which drive the social media strategy and objectives. Based on the metrics described in the social media objectives, we can then measure and evaluate the effectiveness of our efforts. Although evaluating social media ROI seems straightforward, it can be challenging to implement in practice.

According to the 2018 Chief Marketing Officer Survey, almost half of CMOs say that they cannot evaluate the impact of social media on their business. And further, only 16% say that they can show the impact quantitatively. These results reflect the challenge of indirectly connecting social media marketing activities to changes in consumer behaviour. Further, the CMOs did not perceive social media marketing as contributing very strongly to their company's performance, with average ratings below the midpoint of the seven-point scale, ranging from very high impact to no impact. Because social media conversations often occur beyond the direct control or oversight of the company, the outcomes, i.e., changes in consumer awareness, knowledge, or behaviours - can be challenging to measure. The meaning of many of the more direct measures of social media activity, such as likes on Facebook or Instagram, are difficult to link to concrete marketing outcomes.

In addition, because social media activities involve engaging employees throughout the organization in conversation with consumers, isolating the costs associated with a specific social media initiative can be challenging. Still, measuring the impact of social media efforts is essential for two reasons.

- First, an assessment of social media ROI demonstrates where social media efforts are providing value to the firm.
- And second, understanding social media ROI helps us evaluate how to use resources more effectively.

This chapter will present a framework for evaluating social media ROI. You'll see that while there is no magic formula, assessing social media ROI is possible when you start with an unmistakable sense of what you are trying to accomplish. I'll also help you examine how to evaluate the role of paid advertising in generating social media engagement.

In 2018 Lenovo, a company that manufactures and sells computer hardware to businesses and consumers realized that it was losing ground in the business-to-business market. In particular, they saw that a group of younger, tech-savvy and social media active professionals had a more significant impact on the information technology purchase decision.

Was it possible for Lenovo to reach this group of influencers more efficiently and effectively using social media marketing? And how would they assess the return on that investment?

To reach this new group of influencers, Lenovo empowered and engaged a team of employees to share information about the brand and provide thought leadership about technology more generally on Twitter and LinkedIn. According to an article in CMO Innovation, over six months, these efforts resulted in 135,000 pieces of content that were shared, generating 33 million impressions and 62,000 engagements. In addition, they found a 60% increase in Twitter followers and a 115% increase in LinkedIn followers.

How can Lenovo evaluate the return on their investment in this social media marketing effort?

Here is the formula you could use to calculate social media return on investment.

$$\text{ROI} = \frac{(\text{return - investment})}{\text{investment}}$$

You could calculate social media return on investment, or ROI, as a ratio of the revenue attributable to social media, that is, the profit or returns obtained from social media efforts, minus the cost of the investment in social media marketing, to the total investment in social media marketing.

For example, an ROI of 50% suggests that for every dollar spent on social media, there is a net benefit of $0.50. If we invest $100 in social media and the social media return is $150, we will make $50 on that investment.

Calculating ROI allows us to compare the payoffs associated with different marketing investments easily. To use this formula, we need two pieces of information.

First, what is the return? i.e., what is the value of the benefits earned based on social media?

Second, what are the costs associated with this effort? i.e., what is the investment?

In an ideal world, benefits and costs would be measured in the same currency, but as in the Lenovo example, the return on efforts is not always measurable in a dollar value.

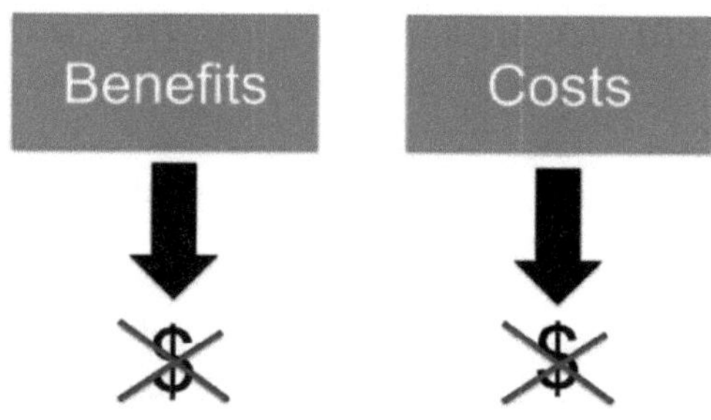

In this case, the outcomes include impressions of content, engagement with content, and the number of followers on social media platforms. To use this formula, you will need to estimate a dollar value associated with these measures.

What is the company's value to the increased level of visibility and interaction?

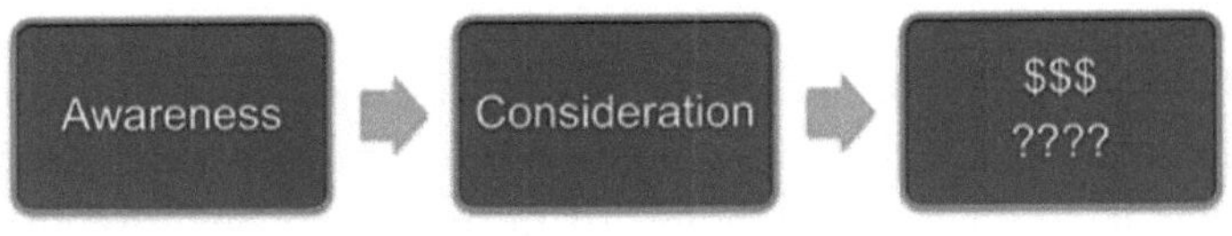

These metrics suggest that social media efforts impacted consumer awareness and consideration, but how do we link those changes to purchase behaviour and the bottom line?

In addition, the cost can be challenging to assess. In the Lenovo example, what should be included in the cost estimate? Some expenses might be relatively easy to track, such as the cost of social technology used to manage the interactions and employee training. Other prices are more difficult to measure. For example, Lenovo uses employees to share content as part of their day-to-day responsibilities, so how should they account for the cost of employees' time in this process?

To calculate social media return on investment, we need to understand the benefits and costs of our social media efforts. Benefits are associated with moving an individual to a particular stage of the consumer purchase funnel. I've noted that it can be challenging to translate these changes to a monetary value. In the next chapter, I will introduce some of the metrics that can assess the impact of our social media efforts.

CHAPTER XVIII

Linking Metrics to Objectives

In the previous chapter, I described a formula for calculating social media return on investment. I recognized that it could be challenging to measure the benefits and costs of social media marketing. In this chapter, I will provide an overview and example of calculating social media return on investment. I will also help you examine how to identify meaningful metrics that reflect the benefits of our social media marketing efforts.

Seven-Step Process

Here is a seven-step process for calculating social media ROI:

1. Start with objectives
2. Identify social media metrics that connect to those objectives
3. Track the appropriate metrics
4. Assign a monetary value to each metric
5. Calculate investment
6. Calculate return or benefits
7. Calculate the ROI and assess

Please note that our business and marketing objectives drive this process. Let me walk you through a specific example.

In Step 1, you will set your objectives

Let's assume that you run a florist shop and would like more people to come into your store. Perhaps you have a free workshop every Wednesday evening that teaches people a different flower-related skill each week (design a bouquet, extend the life of your cut roses, etc.). A certain percentage of people who attend a workshop tend to purchase, so you want to double the number of people who attend the workshop. Currently, an average of 5 people attend each workshop, so your main objective is to get ten or more people to participate in each workshop.

Moving on to Step 2: identify social media metrics that connect to this objective

What are some social media metrics that would be important to you? You could decide to create a Facebook event for each workshop. Metrics include anything you can measure to compare effectiveness against not doing this campaign. One metric is the number of Facebook events per workshop session (in this case, 1 or 0). Other metrics include the number of people who select "I'm going" on the Facebook event, the number who click on the registration link, and the number of likes, comments, or shares the Facebook event received, which reflect an interest in and awareness of the event.

Step 3 involves measuring the outcome

So, you've launched your Facebook events, and the three-month time period has passed. After several weeks of using Facebook events, you've seen that your average attendance at the workshops has doubled (you've met your goal!). In addition, you have tracked consumer engagement with the

Facebook event postings. What is the ROI?

Step 4 is to assign a monetary value to metrics

You will need to assign a monetary value to both the workshop's benefits and costs. To calculate the economic benefits of running the workshop, you will have to consult your business' history. When people attend your workshops, how many purchases while at the store? This information provides a conversion metric--that is, a metric that measures how likely it is for someonc to purchase. You know that, on average, one out of every five workshop attendees makes a purchase and that an average customer spends $15 per visit. Then every individual attendance at your course is worth $3 ($15/5=$3). That means you should spend less than $3 on acquiring each new class member. (Note: If these workshop attendees become repeat customers, you could also consider their future spending in your analysis.)

You might also choose to assign a monetary value to likes, comments, and shares. Attributing attendance at the event to likes, comments and shares are challenging.

Step 5 is to calculate the investment

How much is your social media investment? It would help if you considered the cost of your time. Perhaps setting up a Facebook event takes 30 minutes, and after considering how many hours you work and how much profit you take home, you've calculated that 30 minutes of your time equates to $10. Thus, setting up the Facebook event costs you $10. If you pay to promote the event in Facebook users' feeds, you will need to factor in that cost as well. Perhaps you pay Facebook to promote an event, for example, which costs $25.

You set up 12 Facebook events at $10 cost (of your time) each (12 x $10 = $120), plus you promoted one of those events for $25 ($120 + $25 = $145) That's a total cost of $145.

For Step 6, you must calculate the return.

Historically, you got an average of 5 people at each workshop, but these past three months resulted in an average of 10 people at each workshop. Since the average money spent per person is $3, you likely made an extra $3 x 5 new people x 12 workshops = $180.

Step 7, the final step: calculate your ROI.

ROI = (return - investment) / investment

ROI = (180-145)/145 = about 24%.

Now you have to decide, was it worth it? Is an ROI of 24% sound? For some, that's fantastic. It's a step in the right direction. For others, they might think of ways to get more return on their investment. The best way to evaluate an ROI is to compare it to a benchmark. In this case, a model could be the ROI from previous investment in social media or the ROI in other types of marketing investments.

I've walked you through a simple example of how to calculate social media ROI. In this example, we assumed that the increased attendance at events was entirely attributable to the Facebook event posts (rather than changes in the season or other marketing efforts, for example). This assumption allowed us to calculate the monetary return of our social media effort quickly. In the next chapter, we'll look at how several approaches we can use when the relationship between social media activity and purchase behaviour is not as clear, which is often the case.

Choosing Metrics

Your ability to calculate ROI hinges on identifying the right metrics to track. There is no set of metrics that is important for everyone. The metrics that matter to you depend on your industry, type of business, consumer characteristics, product or service consumption attributes, and, most importantly, the goals you want to achieve. Generally, these goals are linked to moving consumers through the purchase funnel (including post-consumption processes) or creating efficiencies in marketing efforts, such as by providing faster customer service or reducing marketing research expenses.

Therefore, we need to consider which metrics best reflect the objectives we are trying to accomplish. The exhibit below provides some possible metrics associated with specific marketing and social media objectives.

Goal	Key Question	Possible Metrics
Increase brand awareness	How many people see the content?	# of impressions; reach
Change brand perceptions	How do people feel about my brand?	Brand sentiment measures; poll data measuring brand attitudes (e.g., Twitter polls)
Increase brand consideration	How many people engage with the content?	# of likes, shares/retweets or comments; click-throughs without a purpose, saves to wishlists, etc.
Increase brand purchase	How many people buy the product?	Click-throughs to purchase
Increase brand loyalty	Are people spreading the word? Are they saying positive things?	Brand mentions; amount of user-generated content
Increase customer satisfaction	Are questions/issues addressed quickly?	Response time (e.g., how fast you reply to Facebook messages)
Reduce marketing research costs	Can we identify new ideas?	# of ideas generated from social media
Increase sales leads	Can we identify sales prospects?	# of sales leads identified

Here are some key points to remember as you select social media metrics. First, the metrics in this table are suggestive but not comprehensive or mutually exclusive. For example, measures that reflect engagement with content, such as likes or comments, can also reflect increases in brand awareness, as these actions increase the organic reach of the content.

Second, specific metrics are highly dependent on the platform's measurement capabilities. Platforms are continually innovating and developing new features for tracking social media behaviour. Some platforms, such as Facebook and Twitter, provide more ability to track than other platforms, like Snapchat.

Finally, remember that the business objectives should drive metrics--there is not a "one size fits all" formula for selecting metrics. For example, one business may aim to improve sentiment toward their brand by reducing the ratio of harmful to positive tweets. They may care about tweets, mentions, and replies on Twitter a lot more than a click-through or a like. Another business may aim to increase sales on its fall line products by 10% within four months. Click-throughs may matter much more to them; they want consumers to see the links in their tweets and click on those links, leading consumers to the online store. A like or comment may have a much smaller value. A retweet, however, may have more value than a like because it would extend the tweets reach to other groups of consumers who click.

Only you can determine what metrics matter. Don't pay attention to flashy articles online or "social media gurus" that claim to know the top five metrics that matter most.

These seem shortcuts, but they may not lead you to the finish line.

CHAPTER XIX

Linking Metrics to Economic Value

In the previous chapter, you learned the metrics commonly used to measure social media ROI. One limitation of these metrics is that they are not directly linked with consumer purchase behaviour, and therefore do not provide a dollar value for social media benefits. In this chapter, we'll look at two methods that can be used to estimate the economic value of social media benefits.

Let's return to our Lenovo example. Remember that 135,000 pieces of content were shared in the model, generating 33 million impressions.

How can Lenovo calculate the value of those 33 million impressions?

First, Lenovo could calculate a return on impressions. The content that Lenovo posted on social media received 33 million impressions. Suppose we can estimate the relationship between impressions of content and purchase behaviour. In that case, we can calculate the economic value of these impressions, i.e., can we calculate the proportion of people who saw the content that then made a purchase?

For some product categories, data is available to estimate this relationship. For example, The Economist magazine promotes its content to potential customers on Facebook. The Economist knows how many people are exposed to content and how many click through and subscribe to the magazine. In addition, from past subscription data, they can estimate the lifetime value. With this information, The Economist can estimate the economic value of a specific number of impressions on Facebook. Unfortunately, linking impressions and other social media metrics to revenue data is not always so straightforward. This approach works best when purchase data can be directly linked to exposure to an engagement with social media content.

The second approach to estimating the economic value of social media outcomes is to calculate a return on earned media. With this approach, we ask what the brand would have had to pay for advertising to obtain the level of impressions received via social media marketing. In other words, you can calculate an advertising equivalency value for the returns earned via social media. This dollar value, i.e., what advertising would cost to get the same outcome, can then be used to estimate the economic value of social media returns. For example, most online banner display ads are priced using a cost per 1,000 impressions model, or CPM.

If Lenovo attained 33 million impressions via their social media efforts, we can calculate how much it would cost to achieve the same level of impressions using display advertising. If a display ad is priced at $10 per 1,000 impressions, you would have to pay $330,000 for an equivalent number of impressions via display ads. Thus, using a return on earned media approach, we'd assume that this campaign earned Lenovo $330,000 in economic value. Of course, not all impressions are equal. Think about how seeing a display ad while searching for information might differ from seeing content posted on Twitter or LinkedIn. If a trusted, knowledgeable source posts the social media content, consumers might elaborate more deeply on that information and perhaps even comment on it. In that case, an impression gained via social media might have more value than one obtained via another approach.

You already learned the two approaches for estimating the monetary value of social media benefits. The first approach uses historical data about the relationships between marketing outcomes such as impressions or consideration and purchase behaviour to estimate a conversion value, which we refer to as return on impressions. In the second approach, you use advertising or public relations costs to evaluate an equivalency value for our social media outcomes, which we refer to as a return on earned media approach. Both of these approaches have limitations.

Let us examine two more methods for linking metrics to economic value.

Two Approaches to Estimating Social Media ROI

Remember, the 7-step process for estimating social media ROI.

1. Start with objectives
2. Identify social media metrics that connect to those objectives
3. Track the appropriate metrics
4. Assign a monetary value to each metric
5. Calculate investment
6. Calculate return or benefits
7. Calculate the ROI and assess

By now, you would understand the importance of starting with objectives and identifying and tracking metrics linked to these objectives. I also suggested that assigning a monetary value to metrics can be challenging. I described two approaches to estimating this economic value by calculating:

- Return on Impressions
- Return on Earned Media.

Let me help you understand two additional ways to estimate a monetary value for the return on our social media marketing efforts:

- Using Regression Analysis
- Using Experimentation

Regression Approach: Return on Social Media Impact

One frequently used approach is to build a statistical model that describes the relationship between marketing expenditures and activities (including social media expenditures and activities) and outcome variables, such as sales revenues. These models can be used to calculate the return on social media impact. Techniques such as regression analysis are used to provide estimates of how specific marketing tactics and social media engagement metrics are related to sales patterns over time.

To use this approach, the company tracks outcomes of interest, such as sales or the number of leads. These outcomes are the dependent variable, the variable that we are trying to predict. The company can also track expenditures on marketing mix variables such as display advertising and social media campaigns, independent variables, or predictors. Regression analysis can be used to determine the relative effect of each of the marketing mix variables on the dependent variables and provides an estimate of return on investment.

Let's return to our floral shop example from the previous chapter. As the owner of this floral shop, you have tracked how much money and time you have spent on all of your marketing activities, including social media, every week. You also follow the number of visitors to the store and sales results per week. With this data, you could use regression analysis to see if there is a positive relationship between spending on social media activities and visitors to the store and sales, controlling for other marketing expenditures, which will also impact sales.

There are several limitations to this approach.

- First, the effects of marketing mix variables are often not immediate. There is a time lag that must be accounted for in looking at the association between marketing expenditures and outcomes.
- Second, these models do not include all of the variables that might affect sales and thus are often incomplete. For example, the flower shop might spend more money on social media marketing during the seasons when sales would be high anyway, such as Valentine's Day and Mother's Day. Thus, a positive relationship between social media spending and sales could be attributable to increased activity during the holiday season.
- Third, there is a problem of reverse causality - while estimating a return on social media impact via

regression provides insight into the relationship between variables, this approach does not provide insight into cause-and-effect relationships. In other words, while the regression approach might show a positive relationship between social media expenditures and sales, this analysis does not control for other variables that might account for the connection. For example, the flower shop might spend more money during weeks running more popular workshops. Thus, the popularity of the workshops drives the level of promotional spending.

Despite these limitations, estimating a return on social media impact via regression or other statistical models can provide insight into the relationship between social media activities and expenditures and sales or revenue.

Experimentation: A/B Testing

As I mentioned, the regression approach only allows us to see whether two variables are associated, but not necessarily whether there is a cause-and-effect relationship.

Experimentation overcomes this problem by helping to isolate cause-and-effect relationships. Specifically, by using an experiment, we can test the effects of a possible causal variable—such as the amount of money spent on a social media campaign or the type of message used to encourage engagement - on an outcome variable such as sales or click-throughs. To experiment, we manipulate the causal variable and then compare the effects of that manipulation on the outcome variable across different groups of consumers. For example, the floral shop could vary the amount of money spent to promote the workshop events on social media across two randomly selected groups of consumers—with one group receiving "high" spend and another receiving "low" spend on promotion. Comparing the number of event sign-ups in these two groups provides insight into the return on social media expenditures. Because other factors are held constant between the two groups, we can be more confident that the increase in sign-ups is attributable to the amount of money we spent to promote the workshop events. The digital context provides the ability to run simple experiments with fast feedback.

Using experiments requires an outcome variable linked to social media spending, such as a click-through to sign up for an event or make a purchase or impressions of a video.

On the downside, calculating social media ROI in this way often requires a sophisticated understanding of experimental design. Further, because social media results in conversation among consumers, ensuring that a manipulated variable affects only a specific group of consumers can be challenging - that is, the impact of social media can naturally "bleed" across groups.

- When performing an A/B test in a non-social environment, members of the 'A' and 'B' groups are randomly selected, and you can test a feature for an outcome.
- When performing an A/B test in a social media environment - meaning the test involves shared media between people—results can be muddled.

Measuring social media return on investment can be challenging. You can improve your ability to measure social media ROI by having clear objectives, linking objectives to metrics, and measuring what matters. While there is no "fill in the blanks" formula for assessing social media ROI, you can evaluate the financial impact of your social media efforts with some creativity and a thoughtful, logical approach.

CHAPTER XX

Role Of Social Media in Organizations

I hope that, by now, you see that organizations that successfully use social media to meet marketing objectives engage many people, both internal and external to the company, in their social media efforts. Remember, social media is about conversations. While broad participation enhances the value of social media, coordinating and controlling many voices can be challenging.

How can we best manage social media marketing, especially when we have limited ability to control the dialogue?

You learned that social media marketing is driven by brand strategy and informed by ongoing social media listening. In addition, social media marketing involves many decisions about what content to post, where to post it, and how to engage in conversations with consumers. Social media works best when the individuals closest to the customer are empowered to make these decisions quickly. Thus, the processes we use to manage social media marketing need to reflect that so many people throughout the organization are involved. A clear corporate social media policy enables this process.

This chapter will examine how to manage social media marketing best. We'll first learn the general principles underlying social media management and how to develop a corporate social media policy that balances the tension between encouraging broad participation in social media while maintaining consistency and brand voice and adherence to ethical standards. Then we'll explore some specific issues related to social media management, including preparing for and handling a social media crisis and managing online word-of-mouth more generally. Finally, we'll learn some critical ethical issues in social media marketing, including disclosure of sponsorships and privacy issues.

Social media management is an integral part of an organization's business strategy, meaning that it affects and is affected by all aspects of the business. Therefore, it requires a clear policy and code of ethics. The public nature of social media also presents challenges that need timely responses. So, companies must be prepared to engage with customers and manage the brand in a crisis.

Managing Social Media Marketing

Social media marketing engages many voices across the company- that is, it is a distributed function. The distributed nature of social media marketing leads to three key challenges:

- How to manage the tension between engaging many voices and message control;
- How to manage the number and consistency of accounts speaking on behalf of the organization; and
- How to oversee compliance with regulations.

Social Media Policy

It is essential to have a clear social media policy. As a result of the distributed nature of many aspects of social media management, an organization will benefit by creating a thoughtful social media policy. A social media policy is a document that provides rules or guidelines for its people - usually employees - as they engage in social media. A policy can be targeted to those involved in managing social media and those who may work in other areas of the organization who participate in social media marketing as part of their job. Having a social media policy enables employee engagement and can provide some control over sharing and protect the firm against legal risk. As you read the social media policy, ask yourself the following questions.

- Who is this policy targeted towards?
- What are the fundamental rules that govern social media engagement at the chosen firm?
- Do you think this is an effective social media marketing policy statement? Why or why not?

Considerations while developing a social media policy

As you develop a social media policy for your organization, consider the following questions:

1. **Who is this policy targeted to?** The social media marketing staff? All employees? All department heads? For example, at a university, a social media policy can apply to administrators, professors, and students.

2. **What parts of the policy are rules** (e.g., an employee can be fired if they do not adhere to these rules), and which are guidelines (e.g., best practices)? Keep in mind that it may be illegal to require certain behaviours of your employees.
3. **What are the rules specific to your industry?** In your policy reminders, you might choose to include industry rules that employees should be aware of (e.g., practices for compliance in healthcare).
4. **What are some mistakes that have been made in the past?** It can be helpful to include in your policy any guidelines that target weaknesses in the organization. A policy is a living, breathing document. It should be revisited and modified each year to keep it relevant.
5. **What resources can you provide?** There may be people in your organization who would like help in improving their performance. You can list resources within your organization that can help them improve their social media customer service skills or practice writing compliant Facebook posts. Also, help them know where to go when they have an issue. Include contact information and a promise to assist with policy-related matters.

Writing the social media policy

There are no hard and fast rules for writing a social media policy statement. Generally, at a minimum, the social media policy statement will cover the following topics.

- Expectations and guidelines for online behaviour, including:

    - Topics and content to avoid.
    - How to set up an account (individual or affiliated with the company).
    - The need for a disclaimer.

- Confidentiality and privacy - guidelines for what can and cannot be shared.
- Procedures for posting - processes that must be followed before posting and how that might differ for individual accounts versus company accounts.
- Consequences - what can/will happen if policies are not adhered to.

A social media policy is critical in highly regulated sectors, like health and financial services.

How To Manage Word of Mouth

Social media marketing is all about word-of-mouth communication. Consumers might incidentally mention a brand on social media when describing events or activities in their lives, or they could intentionally write a product review and share a recommendation. Word of mouth communication may feel beyond the marketer's control.

How can we best manage word of mouth communication on digital platforms?

Research shows that information shared by other consumers, such as product recommendations, significantly influences purchase decisions. Think about how often you've checked reviews on Amazon before buying a book or TripAdvisor before booking a hotel reservation. Several empirical studies have found that the star ratings of online consumer reviews predict sales.\ These findings raise the question of how actively marketers should manage online word of mouth, such as consumer reviews.

Marketers can influence online word-of-mouth communication in several ways.

- First, marketers can influence where product information is shared. For example, companies can feature a link to their TripAdvisor profiles. Likewise, they can run contests and promotions to encourage consumers to share photos or videos on Instagram or Facebook.
- Second, marketers can influence how much product information is shared. Again, sharing can be incentivized in various ways. For example, because the quantity of online reviews is positively related to sales, retailers can incentivize consumers to post reviews on their online store by offering them the opportunity to win a prize in a sweepstake. Other retailers will encourage sharing by emailing consumers after a purchase or service encounter, requesting that consumers share their experience.
- Third, while more challenging, marketers can attempt to influence the shared content. Controlling content is more complex because the most significant influence on consumer word of mouth is likely to be the quality of the consumption or purchase experience. That being said, companies can help frame the conversation or what is shared. For example, companies can remind consumers of particularly positive experiences and incentivize them to share these experiences on social

media.

- Finally, marketers can respond to online word of mouth. Research conducted within the hotel industry found that hotels generally benefit from responding to online reviews, both in terms of the average star rating and the number of positive reviews received.

While word of mouth communication seems like it would be difficult to manage with forethought, clear objectives, and appropriate resources, marketers can influence the location, amount, and content of the online word of mouth and respond to consumer input as appropriate.

How To Manage a Crisis on Social Media?

What happens when something goes wrong on social media? There are generally two types of crises that arise in social media:

1. A brand crisis is sometimes referred to as a "PR crisis." This is when your brand equity is under attack. Examples range from a negative customer review to a celebrity bad-mouthing a product.
2. A community crisis. This natural disaster impacts your brand and others, including customers, employees, natural resources, and more. A blizzard affecting your city, including your ability to ship products in time, is an example of a community crisis.

Many real crises may also be brand crises for the company, but not all are. A product malfunction is a community crisis—your product's malfunction physically injures users. It is also a brand crisis because it will affect the trust people have in your brand. A hurricane is also a community crisis, but it will not directly affect your brand. It is not your company's fault that the storm occurred. Not responding appropriately to a community crisis can lead to a brand crisis. If you do not respond well in community crises, your lack of appropriate communication can lead to a brand crisis.

How can you prepare for a crisis?

1. **Assess the social media channels that your organization uses** and how consumers can communicate with you in these channels. On Twitter, people can retweet you, reply to you, mention you, and they can even direct message you if they want to. People can write reviews of your business on your Facebook Page, comment on posts, and mention your page on their own private and public Facebook posts. To be prepared, develop a list of all of your channels and the different modes with which consumers communicate.
2. **Assess social media channels your organization is not using.** Don't think that if you don't use a platform, you are safe from the risks of that platform. Consumers will talk about your brand in their social media networks whether or not you are involved. Sometimes (but not always), not being on some networks can exacerbate a crisis because the organization cannot respond.
3. **List all of your stakeholders**—anyone (and anything) that is affected by your business. These stakeholders include customers and users (these may be different; for example, a mother may be the buyer, but the user may

be the child); investors, employees and their families, people who live in the geographical vicinity of your warehouses or stores, the environment (air, water, forests, animals, and so on), the city or community.

4. **Create a social media crisis plan.** In its simplest form, a crisis plan for social media includes a list of all possible crises that could happen. If it is even 1% likely, list it. Create another column for every social media channel that you use. In the cells, write a template message for each scenario. See the below example (the wording in this example may not be appropriate for your audience; please compose your messages that reflect your organization's tone, policies, and community expectations and needs).

What factors should a social media marketer consider in situations of crisis?

- Is this a brand crisis or a community crisis (or both)?
- Who is affected by this crisis? List everyone who is immediately impacted.
- What are the different points of view that these stakeholders may have? Try to see things from their point of view.
- What needs to be addressed immediately?
- Are you being proactive or reactive? Are you reacting to the situation or a specific person?
- Should you respond? If so, should you do so publicly or privately (or both)?
- You may not have all the facts right away. What can you do before you have all the points?

Preparation is critical when dealing with a social media crisis. The framework above can be used to develop your plan for coping with problems in social media marketing. The program requires that you:

1. Identify channels where you interact with consumers and where consumers may post messages about your firm.
2. Identify stakeholders or constituencies that are affected by your business.
3. List possible crises precipitated by internal and external events to the firm.
4. Craft possible responses for each platform and stakeholder for these crises.

This crisis plan should be a living document for your firm, with regular updates and reviews. While no program will be comprehensive, having thought through these issues will facilitate a response, even to unexpected situations.

Business Scenario

You are the social media manager of Mr. Burgers, a fast-food chain with franchised locations across India. Early this morning (before sunrise!), you got a call from one of Shoaib's employees.

You: *Hello?*

Shoaib: *We have a huge problem.*

You: *What's the matter?*

Shoaib: *I woke up this morning, and my phone was buzzing. I've been getting thousands of Twitter notifications. One of our employees, Samir, posted a YouTube video of himself saying all sorts of horrible things about Mr. Burgers, including some lies! He said we always used expired cheese and didn't get a raise he deserved.*

You: *Whoa, slow down; why is your phone buzzing, then?*

Shoaib: *I'm getting all sorts of tweets mentioning us and linking to the video. Lots of people are furious.*

How would you respond to this crisis?

Your response should answer the following questions:

- If you should respond publicly, how? If not, why not?
- What would you do first?
- What steps could you take to prepare for a problem like this if it comes up in the future?

CHAPTER XXI

COVID-19 and Digital Marketing

"In the middle of difficulty lies opportunity. Albert Einstein"

Many see the light at the end of the tunnel. But Covid-19 is far from over. The pandemic has affected all businesses – and marketers need to adapt their digital marketing strategy. Companies have been required to adjust to a new way of life.

Now marketers are asking themselves, "how permanent are these changes?" and "how do I manage the new digital landscape?".

A New Set of Consumers in the Making

The sudden increase of people being indoors has led to a change in lifestyle where consumers have shifted to spending more time online than before. Brands already catering to the 'sofa-surfers' have shown to be in the clear and in some cases have even seen an increase in sales. Traditional offline brands have innovated new online products to adapt to this new way of living. The most crucial factor of the pandemic is the population's health, but there are far more people affected than merely the sick. Businesses feel the effects of the virus, and companies are announcing cutbacks one after another. Marketing departments around the world are noticing the effects as well. Most marketers are at a crossroads, wondering which path to take in such an uncertain future.

Let's look at how marketers adapt to these new circumstances and what you should keep in mind while getting through the current situation.

How Marketers are Responding

Recent research has shown that 61% of marketers are altering their short-term media strategy. However, only 9% are making long-term changes. There is a slight move from offline media to online, as marketers in the same study made clear that they would take a more online approach. This budget shift is not surprising, considering that digital media is consumed at a higher rate due to the online lifestyle of the post-covid consumer.

The New Trend: Flexible Channels

Marketers seeing a cut in budgets will benefit by moving toward cheaper and more flexible channels such as programmatic advertising, where consumer presence and available impressions are increasing. Digital display ads, social media, and online video are channels that most likely will increase in the short-term media plan.

Out-of-home advertising such as billboards will have much lower exposure due to most people staying at home. Event marketing has come to an immediate stop, and we'll likely see that marketing budgets cease or shift towards online ads. However, not everyone sees marketing budget cuts as the solution. Some B2B brands are increasing digital advertising spending to compensate for the leads they otherwise would have picked up at events.

Long-term Concern

An existing concern is that no one knows when the pandemic is over, and everyone can go back to their regular lives. We are seeing how to spend is decreasing in many industries. The travel sector, retail, or events are scrambling to save costs. However, many on-demand online services will likely increase advertising spending, especially online channels. Services such as online food delivery services, streaming, or online news outlets benefit from a higher online presence. These brands will want to take a larger market share in a larger market and increase spending.

What to keep in mind during the pandemic?

The uncertainty of the future is understandable. Nonetheless, this too shall pass. It is essential to stay focused on the long-term and not shy away from new growth opportunities.

Branding works best long-term. However, cutting budget spending too much could negatively impact the brand. Marketers should not forget that there could be an opportunity amid a crisis. Businesses must also prepare for campaigns to reflect the optimism, for popped-up and expanded physical availability to capture resurgence of demand. Ready your promotions and incentives to grab a share of sales when they recover. But above all, understand that weathering and not just surviving, but thriving, through change is what we all do now. That's all our new normal and has been for a while.

Adapt to the New Customer

Consumers spend more time reading or watching the news than ever before. Marketers now have the opportunity to capture more eyeballs by advertising on these popular websites at a lower cost than in the pre-covid period. An online presence has never been as crucial as today for a brand. Therefore-

- Try to treat your daily work like business as usual, but keep it digital.
- Locate your target audience and how their lifestyle has changed, and map out how you should be targeting them.
- Do not underestimate how the coronavirus has changed your customers and how it has affected their demands.

There is no doubt that the Covid-19 has left its mark in history. The question is how much will change and how the world will look when it's all over. Even during a time that feels like a downward spiral – there can be an opportunity to be seized.

CHAPTER XXII

The Road Ahead

While there is no easy answer to this, we will use this final chapter to examine some key trends in digital innovation and their impact on digital marketing. This chapter will present observations and insights from practitioners working at the forefront of digital innovation.

The COVID-19 pandemic halted global economic order, but it managed to speed up digital marketing operations. In fact, throughout the pandemic, many businesses managed to transition to remote work and understood the significance of digital marketing. For many entrepreneurs and small businesses, digital marketing has become an opportunity to gain a competitive edge in the market. But to venture into the new age of digital marketing, small businesses and entrepreneurs have to be broadminded.

Gen Z and Expanding Reach

More Gen Z users will reach maturity, which means businesses and entrepreneurs will have to redirect their digital marketing efforts. Companies don't have to make drastic changes, but the tactics catered to Gen X or boomers will ultimately become redundant. Gen Z wants a memorable experience, which means digital marketing efforts will be more precise and effective. Professional digital marketers believe that Gen Z and millennials will become "the" target audience for most businesses and require a highly responsive and modified approach.

Globalized Shared Mission

The collective efforts in digital marketing have already become quintessential. But more businesses will adopt a shared and global perspective before using new digital marketing tools or executing ad campaigns. In short, a global perspective will allow businesses of all sizes to expand their reach and simplify various processes. Moreover, marketing messages across different digital channels would allow entrepreneurs and small businesses to build trust with the targeted audience. It will also help enterprises to thwart market skepticism and re-establish their value proposition in the market.

SEO, Data Analytics, and Artificial Intelligence

SEO, data analytics, and AI have become part of the digital marketing landscape. As AI evolves, businesses will automate more digital processes and make informed business decisions based on data analytics insights. One report highlights that more than 85% of digital ads will be executed through automation in the foreseeable future. But "how" you collect and render insights from a data analytics tool will also change. More businesses would focus on innovative technologies to categorize audiences and configure ad space through extensive data analysis with automated programmatic advertising in play.

Heightened Personalization

When it comes to personalized targeting, tracking KPIs and other digital marketing tools will continue to play an integral role. Personalized targeting has become a secret ingredient in rolling out effective ad campaigns and communicating with the target audience. Each element of an ad is essential and allows businesses to deliver value via storytelling.

In the new age of digital marketing, entrepreneurs and small businesses will need to be more critical and reflect on previous efforts. For instance, the more precise language of an ad shows the intent and confidence of the brand. And users will opt for brands that are not reluctant about their core message.

The Use of Augmented Reality

When it comes to the tech tools that make it easier for small businesses to communicate with the audience, AR tools are at the top. Many start-ups already use augmented reality technologies to achieve significant growth in the coming years. Most digital marketing experts believe that augmented reality will play a crucial role in the future and help eCommerce businesses set a new path.

Voice Optimization

More dependence on automated digital assistant solutions will allow more definite and objective digital marketing efforts. Whether it's Cortana, Alexa, Google Assistant, or Siri, voice search continues to gain more popularity. More users want the freedom to speak to a dedicated digital assistant directly rather than type manually. What's interesting is that optimizing keywords for voice-based search is entirely different. And that's because when people want to adapt and start using their digital voice assistance, they use keywords and phrases that are more realistic and practical. As the voice recognition capabilities of digital assistants improve, digital marketers will focus on a more different SEO approach to optimize business sites based on voice search. You may not be aware of it, but more than 70% of people with one or more activated digital assistants prefer to use voice commands rather than type the task. The fundamental approach of SEO is identical to voice recognition.

But the spotlight will be on a new style of keywords and phrases that people use in their day-to-day routine. The rise in voice recognition technologies means digital marketers will target more accurate voice search results for ad campaigns and boost SEO efforts. Google concurs that voice recognition of digital assistants is close to 95% accurate. But more precise voice recognition search results mean digital marketers will use more natural long-tail keywords than generic text-oriented ones.

Omnichannel and Integrated Approach

Small businesses and entrepreneurs no longer need to restrict their online presence to a single Facebook page. With more market expectations and consumer needs, companies to be active on various digital channels and platforms. Fortunately, there are already tools like Hootsuite that allow businesses to maintain a unified omnipresence. Companies will integrate their core message and value proposition for the specific target audience on various channels in the coming years. A suitable omnichannel digital marketing strategy will allow more businesses to understand their customers' changing behaviour, location, and preferences.

More Awareness

It would be best to have a massive target audience use digital marketing for lead generation, conversion, or brand awareness. The future of digital marketing is bright because now there is more market and consumer awareness. Businesses can also use a wide range of intelligent tools to collect an ocean of data and make in-depth analyses about their target audience. It's an entirely new way to approach the audience. Extensive market and consumer research allow businesses to leverage untapped opportunities.

Businesses don't need to understand every facet of new technology. Of course, the mechanics of an intelligent tool matter, but businesses that plan to broaden their digital marketing approach will see the most positive results. It is the main reason innovation will become vital for B2C and B2B players.

What makes up a future-proof digital marketing strategy?

A few years ago, what may have been widespread digital marketing practice would become outdated. There is always a paradigm shift that propels businesses and entrepreneurs to post more personalized content, adapt new SEO rules, and embrace intelligent digital technologies when it comes to digital marketing.

Small businesses that want to follow the tide of digital marketing can afford to overlook emerging trends in the space. The key is to determine how a specific direction may change the digital marketing landscape and impact business position. In 2021, the online shopping landscape will become diversified, and ethnic minority users prefer an inclusive approach. Digital marketing has become more than just about click-through rates – it's now about how businesses contextualize emerging trends and approach their target audience for various purposes.

Back to Basics

Of course, all these technological advances are fascinating. Still, we shouldn't lose sight of the basic principles that make for a great marketing strategy and a great company. Employee activation will enable your organization to get the best out of every employee, who will act as ambassadors for your brand and grow sales and conversions genuinely and authentically. That's more effective than any advertising campaign could ever be.

When your employees are engaged, they will themselves act as micro-influencers for your company. Suppose you successfully employ individuals who align with your brand values and help their passion for what you're trying to achieve grow. In that case, they will act as your most dedicated cheerleaders. As our reliance on technology grows, more and more organizations are also realizing they need to be more "human" and must activate the storytelling and organic sharing power of employees – this is the "paradox of AI" as we learn to take our place alongside machines in this brave new world of opportunities.

In the last decade, digital marketing has been through significant upswings. From social media to search engine optimization, digital marketing positively impacts billions of users. With more advanced tools and practices, digital marketing will propel companies to step up their competitive drive in the market. Digital marketing has made it possible for small businesses and entrepreneurs to increase their ROI and roll out effective ad campaigns. In time, the effectiveness of digital marketing practices will reach new heights and allow companies to make the most out of AI, SEO, AR, and VR tactics.

As of now, many digital marketing trends may or may not pan out in the coming years. Unlike the traditional approach, the new wave of digital marketing boils down to customer behaviour. Recent strategic digital marketing efforts will allow businesses to set a new precedent.

Where do you think marketing is going?

Portfolio

Anish K Ravi is the author of Reimagining Marketing. In a corporate and academic career spanning more than 15 years, he has worked across sales, marketing, product, and brand management profiles. He is currently the Professor of Marketing at Chennai Business School. Anish is an academic by choice and shares his marketing perspectives besides being an ardent observer and assiduous annalist of the emerging marketing landscape.

Printed by Libri Plureos GmbH in Hamburg,
Germany